SUCCESSFUL
SYNAGOGUE
ADMINISTRATION

SUCCESSFUL SYNAGOGUE ADMINISTRATION

by IRVING I. KATZ
EXECUTIVE SECRETARY, Congregation Beth El
Detroit, Michigan

and MYRON E. SCHOEN
DIRECTOR, UAHC *Commission
on Synagogue Administration*

Union of American Hebrew Congregations
New York

Preface

FOR MORE THAN thirty years, the Union of American Hebrew Congregations (UAHC) has concerned itself with the management, financing, and programming of the American synagogue. Together with the Central Conference of American Rabbis (CCAR), it created in 1931 the Commission on Synagogue Activities, which undertook study and research and launched a program of practical aid to lay leaders and rabbis in the solution of some of the most pressing problems facing an ancient institution which was attempting to adjust to a new social, economic, and religious climate.

Great impetus to this program was added in 1941, when an organization of synagogue secretaries and executives was founded under the aegis of Irving I. Katz of Congregation Beth El, Detroit. Mr. Katz, a pioneer in his profession and a nationally recognized authority, has served in this field for thirty-five years. In 1955, this group of professional administrators, now known as the National Association of Temple Administrators (NATA) was designated an affiliate of the UAHC. This marked an expansion of the program, which was further accelerated by the creation in 1957 by the UAHC of an Office of Synagogue Administration and the appointment of Myron E. Schoen as its director. In 1962, Mr. Schoen became the director of the newly established Commission on Synagogue Administration of the UAHC and CCAR. Mr. Schoen has been in intimate contact with hundreds of congregations and his weekly column in the *National Jewish Post and Opinion* is widely read.

The manifold committees of NATA and the Commission on Synagogue Administration have undertaken projects and issued publications which have strengthened the contemporary synagogue and made possible not only its expansion but increased its influence on the individual and in the community.

Although the progress has been significant, much remains to be done in the area of efficient synagogue management, dignified and ethical financing and advance planning, so that the contemporary synagogue can intensify its religious and educational impact. Both lay and rabbinic leadership must be alerted to the fundamentals of synagogue administration so that they can be ever ready to meet the dynamic changes of tomorrow.

It is to this end that I deem this book an important contribution to the American synagogue and to its spiritual vitality, and commend it to the attention of all those concerned with its present and future role.

RABBI MAURICE N. EISENDRATH
President, Union of American Hebrew Congregations

Acknowledgments

THE AUTHORS acknowledge at the very outset that this work had its origin in the pioneering efforts of many individuals and several organizations. We are grateful to the officers, executive board, and members of the National Association of Temple Administrators for their confidence in placing this project in our trust and to the Commission on Synagogue Activities of the Central Conference of American Rabbis and the Union of American Hebrew Congregations for recognizing the importance of this endeavor.

We are profoundly grateful for the inspiration of the late Rabbi Jacob D. Schwarz, first director of the Commission on Synagogue Activities, and the guidance of his successor Rabbi Eugene J. Lipman. It was Rabbi Lipman who aided in the planning, followed it through every stage, gave it his frequent attention, and provided invaluable suggestions.

The contributions of members of NATA are significant indeed. We specifically acknowledge the assistance of Frank J. Adler, Kansas City, Missouri; Leo S. Bamberger, Cleveland, Ohio; Irving M. Coburn, Chicago, Illinois; Nathan Emanuel, New Rochelle, New York; Dr. Max Feder, New York City; Julian Feldman, Washington, D.C.; Harold Friedman, Beverly Hills, California; Louis J. Freehof, San Francisco, California; Henry J. Fruhauf, New York City; Leonard Gold, Houston, Texas; Bernard I. Pincus, Boston, Massachusetts; and Samuel Weisberg, Cleveland, Ohio.

We express thanks for the invaluable suggestions of the Reading Committee of the Commission on Synagogue Activities — Frank J. Adler; Dr. Harold M. Faigenbaum, Troy, New York, chairman of the Commission; Dr. Milton F. Gipstein, Schenectady, New York; Rabbi Eugene J. Lipman, Washington, D.C.; Rabbi Ernest M. Lorge, Chicago, Illinois; and Bernard I. Pincus.

In the preparation of the manuscript, we acknowledge the efficient and generous labors of Miss Edith Miller of the Commission on Synagogue Administration; the practical assistance of Mrs. Ethel Held and Mrs. Myron Mendeles in typing; and Mr. Ralph Davis and his staff in the production and proofreading departments of the UAHC for their excellent technical assistance.

Understanding is not only a form of comprehension but a personal relationship marked by love and harmony. For this type of understanding, we express our heart-felt gratitude to our wives and children, who bore patiently with us the labors of many months.

I.I.K.

M.E.S.

Contents

SUCCESSFUL
SYNAGOGUE
ADMINISTRATION

I The Synagogue
Through the Ages

THE ORIGINS OF THE SYNAGOGUE ARE SHROUDED IN OBSCURITY. Scholars are generally agreed, however, that the synagogue as a place of worship developed either during the Babylonian exile (586-538 B.C.E.) or just before the exile. There is no doubt about the fact that synagogues did exist and functioned in Babylon during the exile. As Rabbi Solomon B. Freehof put it, "Though exiled physically, the Jews could not be exiled from the presence of their God."

There are indications that two different types of synagogues developed in Babylon. They set a pattern which was followed over the centuries, even in twentieth century America.

The Jews who came from a particular village in Judea would tend to congregate in one neighborhood in Babylon, for security and mutual comfort. They socialized together, they helped one another in every way — and they met to pray together to their God. Centuries later, when pogrom-ridden East European Jewry flocked to the New World, they proceeded identically to set up synagogues on the Lower East Side of New York, made up entirely of refugees from Pinsk or Bialystok or Budapest. From Babylon to New York, the *Landsmannschaft* synagogue gave to Jews the inner warmth which comes not only from praying, but from praying among people who matter.

A second type of congregation developed simultaneously in ancient Babylon. Just as Jews from a particular village tended to congregate together, so all the tanners tended to set up shop on the same street, all the potters on another, all the butchers on still a third. Though competitors, they had a community of interest which transcended business hours and extended even into the synagogue. And so "guild" synagogues developed; they still exist. In New York there is a Garment Center Synagogue; there is also an Actors' Synagogue. The closeness of economic identification, too, gave additional meaning to prayer in the synagogue.

3

Ancient Administration

No institution administers itself, and the synagogue was and is no exception. By the end of the fifth century, B.C.E., the synagogue was a complex institution with a fairly definite format. Each local synagogue was autonomous, of course, and was related to the central shrine at Jerusalem in only a tenuous one-way manner: the leadership of the local synagogue saw to it that the *ma-amod* (the local delegation) was selected and made its way to Jerusalem three times each year for the required pilgrimages (*r'golim*). Each delegation bore with it not only the requisite sacrifices but also, presumably, the required tithes for the upkeep of the national Temple.

The local leadership consisted of the elders (*z'kenim*), the heads of families. This local council may or may not have numbered seventy. The head of the council may have been elected by the council itself, or may have been appointed by a central authority in Jerusalem (see Ezra 8:17).

The local council had great authority, not only over the functioning of the local synagogue center itself, but also over the social welfare and even military affairs of the community. From the Elephantine papyri we learn of a complex synagogue-centered organization which extended into all manner of community activities.

Early in the evolution of the synagogue as a religious institution, it took on a three-faceted character it still has: a house of prayer, a house of study, and a house of assembly. The educational program immediately took hold as a central one. So important was *talmud Torah* (study of Torah) within the synagogue that the rabbis decided a synagogue could be converted into a school, but a school could not be converted into a synagogue. During this early period, the synagogue also took on an additional area of concern which it still has in most communities: the administration of the cemetery.

The Medieval Synagogue

With the fall of Jerusalem in 70 C.E. and the end of Jewish national life in Palestine, the synagogue became the center of Jewish life. When legal restrictions and economic limitations combined to make synagogue edifices impossible, all the functions of the institution were carried on in private homes or semi-private halls. But the functions were carried on, and they were extensive.

The synagogue continued as the sole prayer center of the people, aside from the Jewish home, and the central educational agency for the young and for laymen. The great *yeshivos* (seminaries), supported by the synagogue-centered community, educated scholars and rabbis. But the synagogue, as house of assembly, performed many other vital communal functions. It was, in fact, the center of the autonomous Jewish community, which was involved in many governmental activities which have now passed into the jurisdiction of civil authorities everywhere. In some countries, the civil authorities maintained close supervision over the Jewish community quite aside from the invariable tax-collection interest of the government. In others, at various times, however, a full measure of autonomy was granted the Jewish community which, in effect, became self-governing.

There was much legal activity carried on within the synagogue, aside from the normal work carried on by the individual internal Jewish court of law, the *bes din*. Legal claims were announced from the pulpit by the reader. When a misdemeanor was to be punished by whipping, the punishment was inflicted in the synagogue, either in private or publicly. When a Jew felt that an injustice had been done him, he had the right to stop the service before the reading of the Torah and demand redress. Even lost articles were announced from the pulpit, and when found were brought to the synagogue to be claimed. On those occasions, in some eras very rare and at other times all too frequent, when excommunication (*cherem*) was ordered for major religious or moral violations, the synagogue was the solemn scene of the announcement. From the tenth century on, this form of punishment was said to have served as a powerful deterrent to lack of discipline within the community.

Each Jewish community had a prison. We do not know of prisons which were directly part of the synagogue. But the offices and activity rooms of the community and its agencies were frequently adjacent to the synagogue, and the prison was sometimes

located there. In other communities, on the other hand, a special
room in the general community prison was allocated to the Jews.

Administration of the Medieval Synagogue

As in ancient times, the autonomy of the local synagogue-centered community was absolute vis-a-vis Jewish communities else-
where or some central Jewish authority. Even the great *geonim*
(title of heads of the academies of Sura and Pumbedita)
of Babylon exercised only an advisory kind of authority. Local
communities consulted them if they wished, and adhered to their
council if they wished. But the local community was sovereign.
As a result, enormous differences of practice and custom developed in various localities.

In each community the *parnossim* were the lay directors of
the synagogue and all its activities — which meant the whole of
the Jewish community. Synagogue and school, poorhouse and hos-
pital, orphanage and old-age home, funds for the redemption of
captives and dowries for brides, slaughter-house and prison — all
were the responsibility of the *parnossim* or *tove ho-ir* (the elite of
the community). Despite their wide-spread responsibilities and
great authority, however, the *parnossim* were always aware of
the weight of community opinion. For the medieval Jewish community was a democratic institution. There were no classes based
upon wealth, social position, or hereditary rights. There was one
standard of prestige: knowledge. The scholar stood at the peak of
the social ladder.

By the eighteenth century, unfortunately, Jewish communal
life took on more of the coloration of the environment, and wealth,
especially property ownership, became all-important for communal prestige. It would be less than honest to try to maintain that
in twentieth century America our standards have become more
traditional or more noble, by and large.

From a very early period, however, the *parnossim* and other
major officials were elected by the community as a whole, usually
on an annual basis. These officials included the head of the com-

munity (known by various titles), the *gaboim* (treasurers), the poor officer, the sick officer, as well as the *parnossim* or *tove ho-ir*.

The number and types of paid officials of the community varied greatly from city to city and from era to era. The *shochet* (ritual slaughterer), *mohel* (ritual circumciser) — who were frequently the same individual — and *chazan* (cantor) were paid at all times. The rabbi and two *dayonim* (assessors or assistant judges) were not paid until the end of the thirteenth century. They earned their livelihood by being artisans, merchants, or professional men (many were physicians), and gave their services to the community as a *mitzvah* (good deed).

The *shamosh* (beadle or sexton) was, in many respects, the most important paid official of the synagogue and community. In a real sense, he ran the synagogue institution. He carried out the sentences of the *bes din* (court), including corporal punishment. He was the public crier, making announcements in the synagogue, proclaiming new *takkonos* (communal laws), even, in many communities, serving as *schulklopfer*, the functionary who went through the streets calling the Jews to prayer by rapping on their shutters. He apportioned honors during the synagogue service — under the watchful eyes of the *gaboim*, to be sure — and thereby exercised enormous communal authority. He kept records for the community — births and deaths, especially the latter for purposes of *yahrzeit* (anniversary of death) and the memorial contributions which, even centuries ago, augmented the budget of the *kehillah* (Jewish community).

For the most part, however, the varied activities of the synagogue and community were financed by taxation, levied legally by the *parnossim* from every Jew. The taxing power constituted the chief source of authority over the individual citizen, and it was used. In addition to community taxes, every Jewish citizen was called upon at least once a year for a contribution to each of the many charitable and functioning societies within the synagogue-community structure. Gradually, over the centuries, these philanthropic societies assumed a semi-autonomous status within the synagogue-centered community.

In addition, private ownership of synagogue pews was universal and constituted a source of initial revenue for the synagogue. Pews could be bought, sold, and mortgaged. Not infrequently a Christian owned synagogue pews, as a result.

The legal framework within which the community functioned was, of course, rabbinic law. When procedural or substantive laws were needed to meet specific community problems they were promulgated as *takkonos* by the *parnossim*. These always had the approval of the rabbi, and were binding upon the community.

Takkonos covered all aspects of communal and individual life, from tax rate to cemetery administration. The latter, incidentally, was then, as now, a complicated aspect of synagogue administration and the source of many headaches for the *parnossim* and professionals alike. Over the centuries, one unusual problem developed in connection with the cemetery which was solved, by *takkono,* in an unusual way. Old Jewish communities began to run out of burial space in the very limited land granted them for cemetery use. Rabbinic authority and the community leadership combined finally to permit "vertical" burials; that is, the covering of one layer of graves with enough earth to permit the burials of a second group of dead above. In the old cemetery in Prague, many layers of graves exist in one section.

The American Synagogue

Until a little more than a century ago, the American synagogue was generally a carbon copy of its European parent. Students of synagogue life in the seventeenth, eighteenth, and early nineteenth centuries will find fascinating and charming material in the minutes of our American synagogues. Both the American Jewish Historical Society and the American Jewish Archives have published documents containing some of the details of the synagogue-communities as they started to develop in the New World, beginning with Congregation Shearith Israel (Remnants of Israel) of New York. Both the Sephardic (Spanish and Portuguese) and early Ashkenazic (German) synagogues followed completely the overall pattern of European Jewish life — until the German-Jewish immigration flood of the middle nineteenth century. Then a number of changes began in synagogue life which changed fundamentally the nature of the American synagogue, and consequently its administrative procedures.

First, over a period of several decades, the synagogue gave up almost all its traditional functions except the conduct of worship services and the education of young children. For reasons that are complex, by 1900, the synagogue ceased to be the center of the Jewish community, its core institution. Secular agencies, unconnected in any way with the synagogue, on occasion even antagonistic to it, took over full responsibility for all aspects of social welfare, health, community relations, and even, in some communities, the cemetery. As a consequence, the synagogue's Board of Trustees became administrators of a vastly simpler institutional set-up.

Second, the whole *kehillah* idea collapsed in the individualistic air of nineteenth century America, and American Jewry became an organized (often over-organized) anarchy. The synagogue, consequently, had to concern itself only with its members — but it also had to get and keep members. The administrative implications of this fact have been many and serious.

Third, primarily as a result of the pervasive influence of American Protestantism, the functions of the rabbi have changed fundamentally in the United States. No longer is he a teacher and judge; instead, he is required to be a combination of teacher and pastor, administrator and radio-TV artist, ambassador and psychologist, scholar and business executive, officiant, orator, and fund-raiser. Because, for better or worse, the American synagogue revolves around its rabbi, these fundamental changes in rabbinical status and functions have left their mark on the synagogue institution itself.

Fourth, the growth of Reform and Conservative Judaism in the United States has had major effects upon the nature of the synagogue, even of the Orthodox synagogue. From architecture to office management, the structure of the synagogue has been profoundly affected by the Liberal movement in Judaism.

The implications of these changes were gradually felt in American synagogue life. At first, more and more power became centralized in the Board of Trustees, usually composed of the more affluent members of the congregation. They administered the

synagogue. Even large synagogues in metropolitan centers needed only a rabbi, cantor, sexton, and perhaps one clerical worker.
In Reform Judaism both the cantor and sexton disappeared in
many communities many decades ago.

But since 1900 it has become increasingly apparent that the
American synagogue must reflect several basic premises of American life generally, and increasingly it has done so.

First, the synagogue is becoming more democratic. Congregational committees function more effectively and involve more
and more members of the congregation. Wealth no longer controls many synagogues as tightly as it did two generations ago.
Congregational meetings are held more frequently, and valiant
efforts are made to involve the members in vital congregational
policy-making and administration.

Second, synagogue administration has become a recognized
science. No longer does the president run the synagogue's administration and the rabbi its program. Effective professional
staffs increasingly exist to give the complex synagogue institution
the kind of business-like and dynamic program and administration Americans have come to expect and appreciate.

The temple executive is the hub of this approach to synagogue
administration. He first appeared on the scene early in the twentieth century. The late Samuel Berliner had been associated with
Temple Beth El (House of God), which consolidated with Congregation Emanu-El (God Is With Us) of the City of New York in
1927, as early as 1910; S. D. Schwartz has been executive secretary
of Chicago Sinai Congregation since 1914. They were among the
first to become professional synagogue administrators, and pio-
neered in the techniques and procedures of scientific administration. They were followed by more and more executives, untrained
specifically in synagogue administration, but with experience in
executive management of business and industry, secretarial duties, even a number of ex-sextons, ex-funeral directors, as well as
in recent years from Jewish communal organizations.

In April, 1941, following protracted correspondence and nego-
tiations, the National Association of Temple Secretaries was organized in Detroit on the initiative of Irving I. Katz, and on April
30th of that year was chartered by the Union of American Hebrew

Congregations as an agency of its Commission on Synagogue Activities. In 1955 the NATS became an affiliate of the UAHC itself. In 1959 it adopted the name National Association of Temple Administrators.

The Conservative movement in Judaism followed with the organization of the National Association of Synagogue Administrators in 1947.

These organizations have performed vital functions in the exchange of information and ideas, in developing professional standards, in the publication of research studies and other data, and in many other services not only to their members but to their movements generally.

Over the years, an American synagogue pattern has been developing and now appears to have taken firm form. An alert, concerned, informed congregational membership is at its center, with the Board of Trustees and an extensive network of congregational committees carrying out congregational policies and projects. The professional staff consists of the rabbi (plus one or two assistants in larger congregations), the cantor, the temple administrator, a full or part-time educational director, professional religious school teachers, and, in larger congregations, specialized personnel for youth activities and other programs. The synagogue is financed by annual dues payments by the membership on a graduated scale. Increasingly, this one annual dues figure covers the full operating budget of the congregation. Laymen and professional alike exert their energies not alone that the synagogue institution may function effectively, but mostly in order that the synagogue may in fact fulfil its traditional purposes for all its members: the worship of God, the study of His law, and assembly to fulfil in human relationships His will.

EUGENE J. LIPMAN
Rabbi, Temple Sinai, Washington, D.C.

II The Synagogue
as an
Administrative Unit

THE CLOCK ON THE WALL OF THE SYNAGOGUE BOARD ROOM SHOWED it was well past midnight and the weary trustees welcomed the call for adjournment after more than three hours of reports and heated discussion. It had been the routine monthly meeting of the Board of Trustees — routine in that much of the time had been consumed on items such as approving the payment of bills, the condition of the lawn, and the parking facilities. No time had been available, unfortunately, for the discussion of matters pertaining to the religious life of the congregation or its educational program. As one trustee wearily remarked: "We never seem to be able to find the time for these important things any more."

The multiplicity of activities in the contemporary synagogue has made it a complex organization and has placed a heavy burden on the shoulders of its spiritual leader, the rabbi, and on its lay leadership, the officers and trustees. Our lay leadership, composed largely of business and professional men and women, accustomed in their own personal endeavors to an orderly flow of authority and decisions, seem to be frequently disturbed by their inability to "get things done." Too often we find that the capable and devoted trustee becomes discouraged with the constant preoccupation of the Board with routine matters which absorb so much of its time and energy and excludes substantive discussions of the basics of Jewish life; worship, education, and ethical concepts.

The inability to see clearly the administrative outlines of the various groups and organizations which make up our present-day synagogue tends to create that feeling of duplication, overlapping, and working at cross purposes about which we hear so much. To understand the complex structure of the congregation then becomes one of the most important objectives in synagogue administration. Once we have this composite picture in sharp, clear focus, it becomes possible to comprehend the administrative

12

structure so that the synagogue trustees may devote their time and energy to the primary purpose of strengthening Judaism for our congregants.

By tradition the synagogue has a threefold purpose. First and foremost, it serves as a *bes ha-t'filo,* a "house of worship." Second, it must be a *bes ha-midrosh,* a "house of study"; and third, it must serve as a *bes ha-k'neses,* a "house of assembly." To carry out these purposes, the synagogue of today finds itself involved in extensive programming. So diverse and so complex has it become in larger congregations that they have found it necessary to call upon the professional or "specialist." Hence we find in a great many congregations that in addition to the rabbis and cantor, the trustees have found it necessary to engage a full-time professional administrator, an educational director or principal, and a program or youth activities director for the many facets of its cultural and social program.

We are concerned in this volume primarily with the administrative aspects of the modern synagogue and with the application of the theories and practices of efficient business technique. There are those who will look askance when one tries to relate the practices of modern business management to a religious institution. However, our spiritual leaders, the rabbis, bear a heavy burden of pastoral, educational, and communal responsibilities. It is imperative, therefore, for a Board of Trustees to apply tested administrative procedures to assure the successful functioning of all the forces and energies of the congregation so as to bring to its members the richest and most satisfying experiences of our religious heritage.

It is universally agreed that synagogue administration falls generally within the sphere of lay leadership. Today, as in all our long history, the layman's responsibilities and predominance in this area are accepted. Synagogue trustees and officers will share with the rabbi the responsibiility of planning for the spiritual growth of the congregation, but the success of the entire program will usually have a direct relationship to the effectiveness of the lay leadership in managing the business affairs of the congregation. If the financial and administrative affairs of the congregation are on a sound business basis, the time and energy of the rabbinic and lay leadership may then be more fully devoted to the primary purposes of the congregation.

It is the responsibility of the officers and trustees to evolve an organizational set-up that will assure not only an efficient synagogue, but one that will involve the maximum participation by its members and thus give these members the maximum in inspiration and service. It is not a crowd of people with a few leaders that we seek in striving for good administration in the synagogue, for recourse to the dictionary indicates that a crowd with a leader also defines a "mob."

A well-administered organization must have a combination of the following:

1. A thorough knowledge of the goals or ends desired
2. A recognition of responsibility
3. A delegation of responsibility
4. Effective techniques of action and supervision of action.

In every congregation there is a reservoir of energy, skills, and devotion. These "natural resources" often go untapped or lie fallow because we do not have the proper organizational set-up to convert them into constructive and creative channels. For the congregational leadership to provide this motivation and direction it must first understand the administrative picture.

Consider the apparatus of a newly-formed congregation. As in early American political history, the ideal arrangement for governing this fledgling institution would be the "town meeting" of New England lore. At regular intervals the entire membership of the congregation could meet and proceed to discuss and decide all issues of mutual concern. While this remains the essence or ideal of democratic procedure, we find that the average synagogue soon outgrows this apparatus just as the average American community has done over the past century. What the town meeting lacked was the individuals to carry on the day-to-day responsibilities of the organization as that organization assumed increasingly complex and time-consuming activities. In the synagogue, too, we needed individuals charged with the responsibility of carrying out the program. A step up the ladder had to be made, and here, too, the congregation has followed the pattern of our political history. The next step was for the organization democratically to elect officials for stated terms of office.

The Constitution and By-Laws — The Organic Law

To preserve the democratic aspects of complex government, the citizenry generally adopted an organic law which specifically delineated the powers of its chosen officials and reserved certain powers to an elected body of representatives. This is known as the division of executive and legislative power. The organic law is the constitution and by-laws.

All congregations, in drafting this organic law, designate a body empowered to act in the name of the membership between congregational meetings. This body may be known as the Board of Trustees, Executive Council, or Board of Directors. It generally meets once a month on a stipulated day. The powers and duties of this body are generally very broad, embracing the complete management of the property and affairs of the congregation with the power to do all things necessary to carry out the purposes of the congregation and to promote its welfare. It is always subject to the final authority of the plenary congregational meeting, however. Its powers are not confined to the business affairs of the synagogue; that is, the raising of funds and payment of financial obligations. Its duties include the obligation to evolve and implement programs that carry out the spiritual, cultural, and educational objectives of the synagogue. Its obligations extend to every congregational aim and interest. The broader its attitude in this respect, the greater will be its impact on the activities and relationships of congregational life.

The constitution and by-laws of the synagogue should be written in such language as to make their meaning and interpretation clear to all. Clarity of wording is an indispensable requirement. While this may sound elementary, experience has shown that failure to do so has subsequently involved congregations in considerable controversies and complications in trying to determine the meaning of certain constitutional provisions.

The primary purpose of a constitution should be to serve as an instrument that will carry out the wishes and desires of the membership and not obstruct or put shackles on its ability to express its will. Procedural machinery should be, in the new congregation, of the simplest nature, so that all may have access to it in their efforts to participate in synagogue life.

At the outset the document should reflect the fact that the congregation is related to its national organization. In the case of Reform congregations, it will indicate its relationship to the Union of American Hebrew Congregations and that it will accept the guidance of the UAHC and the Central Conference of American Rabbis in its religious practices. In addition, its provisions should touch upon the following major areas:

Membership — Age limitations should be fixed in such a way as to provide for the earliest opportunity of membership for the young men and women of the community.

Voting — In family memberships, consideration should be given to granting the privilege of voting to both husband and wife.

Dues and Assessments — Broad flexibility is the key phrase in this area, permitting the Board and the membership to meet the financial needs of the congregation by the most democratic and sound institutional practices that may be available.

Officers and Board — Provisions should be made to limit tenure of office in order to afford opportunity for all to lend their leadership abilities to the progress of the synagogue while at the same time assuring that experience and devotion will always be accorded recognition and utilized.

Election of Rabbi — This should be in conformance with statutes of the particular state and should give recognition to nationally suggested procedures, like those adopted by the Union of American Hebrew Congregations and the Central Conference of American Rabbis, with provisions regulating tenure, pension, and the clarification of the relationship of the trustees and the congregation to the rabbi.

Fiscal Period — Efforts should be made to fix this in such a manner that the annual budget of the congregation may be submitted at the annual membership meeting for approval. It is recommended that the fiscal year begin following Confirmation (Shovuos) or about July 1 of each year.

Auxiliary Groups — The establishment of these groups and the definition of their role and relationship to the synagogue and its program are vital.

Standing Committees — Provision should be made to establish permanent committees to cover the major areas of synagogue activities, program, and administration.

Personnel — Care should be taken to define the authority to engage and establish the terms of employment for the entire staff.

Amendments — Changes and additions to the constitution and by-laws should be in such a manner as to provide both for the growth and expansion of the synagogue and readily to correct situations which have proven to be a hinderance to its progress.

Organizational Structure

The need for purposeful coordination in the administration of the synagogue may not seem of great import at first, for its organizational structure will be simple and look very much like this:

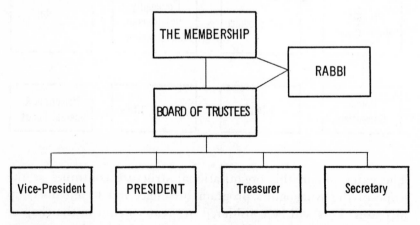

With the growth of the congregation and the expansion of its program will come the addition of affiliates and the addition of many committees. Concomitant with this growth should be the evolution of its organizational and administrative structure. Thus, the

medium-sized congregation may have an organizational chart
which looks like this:

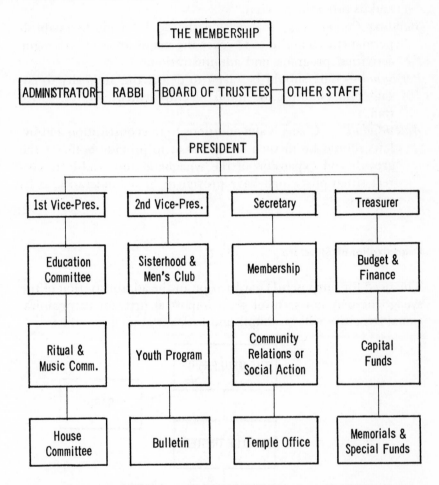

The extension of this organizational structure continues as the
scope of the synagogue's program broadens and its membership
increases. This will be considered in greater detail in the chapter
devoted to committee structure. However, to appreciate fully the
administrative structure, the following is a sample organizational
chart for a large congregation:

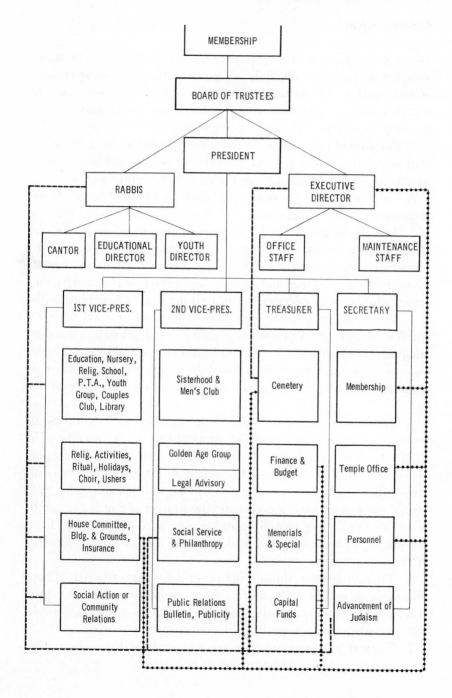

Basic Principles

While no authoritative set of administrative yardsticks or standards has as yet been officially adopted in the field of synagogue
administration, the following principles would receive wide ac-
ceptance and are generally recognized as being in accordance with
the best experience of our congregations:

1. The role of the contemporary synagogue in the modern American scene as a house of prayer, house of study, and house of assembly must be constantly emphasized and reemphasized.

2. The program of the synagogue must be planned to satisfy the
vital needs of the congregants and thus enlist their participation.

3. The synagogue must be soundly organized. This would include a clear distinction between policy-making and execution;
cooperative and creative relationships between Board and staff;
division of labor; clear and definite assignment of authority and
responsibility; and effective coordination of all synagogue units.

4. The synagogue must operate on the basis of good working
conditions and sound personnel practices. Staff personnel must be
adequate in quantity and quality. Employees should be paid adequate salaries and provision should be made for fringe benefits
normally provided in business enterprises and for security in old
age.

5. The synagogue's funds should be regarded as trust funds, to
be administered with a sense of stewardship to the membership
from whom the funds are received. The synagogue should operate on the basis of an annual budget; it should have an adequate
accounting system; its accounts should be audited annually by a
competent professional accountant; the sources of funds and methods of money-raising should be in keeping with the dignity of the
synagogue. Provision should also be made for the future security
of the synagogue.

6. The synagogue should maintain adequate records. These
should be accurate, as comprehensive as necessary for the purpose, yet as simple as possible, filed so as to be readily accessible
when needed, and properly protected and safeguarded.

7. Clerical and maintenance services and facilities should be
adequate in quantity and efficient in operation.

8. The synagogue should be an active and contributing participant in the community and should concern itself with all living issues that affect Jews or Judaism everywhere.

9. All who are officially connected with the synagogue should develop attitudes and methods of work which will build sound public relations. The synagogue should have a definite program of education and interpretation. The synagogue should seek to develop a constituency which will have a real understanding of the needs which the synagogue is trying to meet, and of the synagogue's objectives, services, and problems.

10. The work of the synagogue should be characterized by a basic desire to serve human beings; an understanding of the individuals whom it seeks to serve, and of their needs; a spirit of freedom, unity, and democratic participation in a common adventure in human service; and a sense of creativeness, progress, and growth.

11. Once a year, the synagogue should put itself to the test of a self-appraisal, which would take stock of such matters as the successes and failures of the past year, the present status of the synagogue and its program, its strengths and weaknesses, its current problems, and the next steps that it ought to take.

REFERENCES

BRAMER, J. C., JR., *Effective Church Business Management,* Westminster Press, 1960.

CASHMAN, ROBERT, *The Business Administration of a Church,* Harper & Bros., 1937.

LEACH, WM. H., *Handbook of Church Management,* Prentice-Hall, 1958.

SCHOEN, MYRON E., *Administration in the Contemporary Synagogue,* UAHC, 1958.

SCHWARZ, JACOB D., *ABC of Synagogue Administration,* UAHC, 1937.

———*The Life and Letters of Montgomery Prunejuice,* UAHC, 1957.

III The Role
of the Board
of Trustees

THE HIGHEST AUTHORITY IN THE CONGREGATION IS THE MEMBERSHIP itself. When it meets, it has the power to take over-all and conclusive action in matters pertaining to its organization and activities. For day-to-day administrative purposes, it delegates certain of its powers to a governing body usually designated as the Board of Trustees. This Board is elected by the members of the congregation and its powers and duties are prescribed in the constitution. As a general rule, the prerogatives of the Board encompass the complete management and control of the property and affairs of the congregation, excepting such matters as are reserved for the decisions of the members of the congregation themselves by state law and/or the constitution of the congregation. The Board is usually empowered to do all things necessary to carry out the objectives and purposes of the congregation and to take any action deemed advisable to promote its welfare.

How the Board of Trustees conceives its functions under these general provisions and how it uses the broad powers conferred upon it by the constitution and by-laws is most important. Experience has shown that if the Board confines its duties exclusively to the "business side" of congregational management, the consequence will be a passive or indifferent attitude on the part of the members of the Board toward the spiritual and educational objectives of the congregation. If the Board, on the other hand, regards its function to be not only to exercise control over all congregational property and to make the synagogue financially secure, but to be concerned as well with its aims and objectives of a house of study, prayer, and assembly, the effects of such a broader attitude on the work of the rabbi and the other members of the professional staff, as well as on the relationships and activities of every congregational department and auxiliary organization, will be immediately apparent. Such an interest in policy and program, and a more active participation in the life of the congregation on the part of the trustees, both individually and collectively, will be an encouragement to the membership at large and a valuable help to the professional staff. A BOARD THAT SHARES WITH ITS RABBI THE RESPONSIBILITY OF PLANNING, APPRAISING, AND ADVANCING THE SPIRITUAL GROWTH OF THE CONGREGATION AND OF INTENSIFYING THE JEWISH LIFE OF ITS MEMBERS IS A PREREQUISITE TO A SYNAGOGUE WHICH SUCCESSFULLY FULFILS ITS PURPOSE. This neither challenges nor circumscribes the leadership of the rabbi, without whose knowledge, insight, and inspiration the best laid plans of the lay leaders would collapse. On the contrary, it may direct attention to that leadership, and may go far to make it potent and effective.

Functions of the Board

Every congregation is autonomous and is governed by its own Board of Trustees. The Board makes decisions at its meetings on religious and fiscal matters affecting the welfare of its own congregants as well as the future of American Jewry. Consequently, it makes a great deal of difference as to who serves on the Board of a congregation. Happily, a concern for the quality of the membership of Boards of Trustees is on the ascendency. There is mounting evidence that our congregations are taking an ever-closer look at their Boards. Furthermore, it is heartening that the Boards themselves, individually and through regional institutes and seminars for congregational trustees, are becoming more and more conscious of their responsibilities and are seeking ways to improve their effectiveness in the synagogue.

In order to establish certain criteria for Board membership, we must first ascertain what are the specific responsibilities of a Board member in the contemporary synagogue. An acknowledged authority on synagogue administration, Rabbi Jacob D. Schwarz, in *The ABC of Synagogue Administration,* suggests the following:

1. To exercise management and control of the synagogue property.

2. To be responsible for the solution of all problems relating to membership and dues.

3. To manage the finances, operating on a planned budget.

4. To elect members to the congregation in accordance with its constitution and by-laws.

5. To determine and assess all dues and to prescribe all privileges of membership in the congregation, and to make any special dispensations regarding them.

6. To engage such salaried personnel as necessary and to fix their compensation.

7. To study the congregational constituency from the point of view of personal participation and needs, with a view to converting nominal members into supporters and active participators.

8. To inform themselves thoroughly on the work of all congregational affiliates and activity units — Brotherhood, Sisterhood, Youth Groups, Couples Clubs, etc.

9. To familiarize themselves thoroughly with the synagogue's school and other congregational means of Jewish education for youth and adults.

10. To take measures to insure enrollment in the synagogue school of all eligible children in the congregation.

11. To plan with the rabbi the religious, educational, and social program of the synagogue.

12. To devise ways and means to restore the synagogue as the center of Jewish life.

13. To devise ways and means of increasing opportunities for Jewish fellowship in the synagogue.

14. To share with the rabbi the required pastoral and contact work as well as the duty to represent the congregation in the community in civic and communal affairs.

15. To set the example in participation in divine services as well as in all other phases of congregational life.

Rabbi Julius J. Nodel evolved "Ten Commandments for Board Members."

1. Thou shalt know why thy temple exists and annually review why it should.

2. Thou shalt interpret the place and function of thy temple to the community and not hide its light under thine indifference.

3. Thou shalt not accept the name of thy office in vain.

4. Conduct thy meetings through joint thinking; accept its decisions with grace; and deal with rabbi, educational director, executive secretary, and administrative staff as partners.

5. Thou shalt keep far enough ahead of the membership to be progressive and close enough to it to be practical.

6. Thou shalt spend thy treasury for the temple and save it not for the record.

7. Thou shalt face budgets with courage, obligations with optimism, deficits with dismay, and recover quickly from a surplus.

8. Thou shalt give money, help get it, or both.

9. Thou shalt not be a false witness of the ideals which thou holdest up to others, but through attendance at services and participation in all activities thou shalt set an example to thy spouse, thy son, thy daughter, and everyone who enters thy temple's gates.

10. Thou shalt be part of a tradition, but eager to improve it.

Policy Making Plus

A lay leader, Monte A. Feinstein, of Sinai Temple, Springfield, Massachusetts, has said:

> Every generation gets the leaders it deserves. This may or may not be so, but it certainly is true that communities throughout the country have realized, with increasing awareness, that the quality of leadership is crucial to its progress. We at Sinai must develop programs for interesting the most able potential leaders in temple service, and develop procedures for building the experience necessary for top-level responsibility.
>
> You have just been rewarded — rewarded for your work, or your giving, or your leadership, or for a dozen other things which may have motivated your election.
>
> I believe the first thing a temple Board member must learn is that a position on the Board is not its own reward, but rather the beginning of learning and working and maturing — if you would do this job as well as you'd like.
>
> To some, Board membership in a community organization

may mean the realization of a deep-seated personal ambition. For others, it represents a unique opportunity to contribute one's talents to the service of the temple and community. Being a Board member means a great deal more than attendance at meetings. One must, of course, attend meetings, for only in this way is it possible to acquire the spirit of our organization and obtain the information as to its activities.

It is necessary that a Board member be fully informed, because he is the means through which the activities of our organization are interpreted to the community. Board members should acquaint themselves with the activities of similar groups in this city, so that they can be better informed on what transpires outside our own organization.

It is incumbent that all Board members attend all religious services as well as functions. Be on hand to welcome and well-wish a stranger, a new member, and your friends. Your presence means so much to the success of our institution.

Lastly, and so important, Board members must learn to be liberal in their contributions, and to enjoy the feeling and satisfaction of being first to do his or her part.

Criteria for Board Membership

In the light of these comments, what kind of congregants are best suited for Board membership and what personal qualifications should they possess?

The most important qualifications to seek in a Board member are:

1. A knowledge of and a commitment to Judaism.

2. A conviction that the synagogue has a vital role to play in the Jewish and general community.

3. The desire to understand and the ability to advance the basic purpose, philosophy, program, and policies of the synagogue.

4. An attitude that the synagogue can and should be run efficiently.

5. A sense of communal responsibility.

6. Previous or current experience as a committee member,

Board member, or officer of the synagogue's auxiliaries and/or service in the Jewish and general community.

7. Potential capacity for leadership.

8. Sound judgment.

9. Open-mindedness.

10. Ability to work cooperatively as part of a team.

11. Ability to participate in discussion and function effectively at Board meetings.

12. Willingness to work in partnership with the rabbi and professional staff.

13. Desire and readiness to give time and assume responsibility.

14. Special abilities that can contribute in specific ways to the synagogue program.

15. Views representative of a segment of the congregation.

16. Example in support of the synagogue, according to financial ability.

If synagogues will seek and develop Board Members with these qualities, we shall be building the kind of Board which will work in consonance with the new concept of a dynamic and forward-looking Judaism in America. Of course, no synagogue expects to find each Board member possessed of all these qualifications in full degree as he begins his Board service. If he is helped, he will learn to grow on the job. Board members are made, not born.

REFERENCES

BLUMENTHAL, LOUIS H., *How to Work with Your Board and Committees*, Association Press, 1954.

BRODSKY, IRVING, *Manual for Board Members*, National Jewish Welfare Board, 1957.

COHEN, NATHAN E., *The Citizen Volunteer*, Harper & Bros., 1960.

CROSSLAND, WELDON, *Better Leaders for Your Church*, Abingdon Press, 1955.

DEMOREST, CHARLOTTE K., *The Board Member's Manual*, National Publicity Council for Health and Welfare Services, 1951.

DOLOFF, EUGENE D., *The Efficient Church Officer*, Fleming H. Revell Co., 1949.

FELDMAN, JULIAN, *The Challenge to the New Board Member,* UAHC, 1959.

SCHWARZ, JACOB D., *New Trustees for a New Age,* UAHC, 1938.

SORENSON, ROY, *The Art of Board Membership,* Association Press, 1950.

TRECKER, HARLEIGH B., *Building the Board,* National Publicity Council for Health and Welfare Services, 1954.

IV Developing
an Effective
Board of Trustees

Orientation of New Board Members

THE CONGREGANT WHO HAS COMMITTED HIMSELF TO BOARD MEM-
bership is interested in serving as effectively as he can. The new
Board member is anxious to find a useful role as soon as possible
and to demonstrate his abilities. If the synagogue Board is working effectively as a group, he desires to be accepted as part of the
working group. It goes without saying that proper orientation and
preparation are vital prerequisites for a satisfactory experience.

Every new Board member should have the opportunity for a
period of "basic training" and orientation. He must be given information about the synagogue's needs and problems, its services,
and the organization of the Board. This information will help him
develop the awareness, attitudes, and skills required for his effective service. After the new Board member has obtained a basic
orientation, his growth and development can occur through "on
the job" learning.

In subject matter and approach, the orientation should be
adapted to meet the needs of the individual, varying with his
knowledge of the synagogue and the community, and with his experience as a Board or committee member in other organizations.

Orientation may be carried on in a formal group comprising
several new Board members, or informally with individuals. The
responsibility for orienting new Board members is shared by the
officers, key committee chairmen, the rabbi and the administrator, the educational director, and other staff members.

The orientation should impart information about the following:

1. Programs and policies of the synagogue and its auxiliary
organizations.

2. The relationship of the congregation to its national institutions.

3. The organization of the synagogue and its significant operating procedures.

4. The functions of the Board; administrative relationships between the Board and its committees, the Board and the rabbi, the Board and the professional staff, and the Board and the membership.

5. The financing of the synagogue.

The orientation, as a beginning experience, can set a tone for mutual understanding and warmth of relationship between the new Board member, the synagogue's officers, the rabbi, and staff. In this initial period, the assignment of duties to the new Board member should not be hurried.

Many types of records and reports should be made available to the new Board member to help inform him about the work of the synagogue. It is recommended that, following his election, a kit be provided containing the following:

1. Highlights of the history of the congregation.

2. The constitution and by-laws.

3. The Annual Report for at least two previous years.

4. An outline of major events for the coming year.

5. The current budget as compared with receipts and disbursements for the past fiscal period.

6. The Organizational Chart of the synagogue.

7. Literature relating to the work of the congregation's national institutions.

8. A directory of officers and Board members (name, business and home address and phone number, occupation, date of expiration of term of Board member).

9. A directory of officers and Board members of auxiliary organizations (name, business and home address and phone number).

10. A committee roster and brief outline of major responsibilities.

11. A directory of the professional staff.

12. A schedule of forthcoming national and regional conven-

tions of the congregation's national institutions as well as state and regional institutes for Board members.

The On-Going Education of Board Members

In this scientific and technological age, all of us are called upon to devote countless hours to preparing ourselves for whatever work we propose to do in society. There are no longer any areas of modern life where training can be dispensed with. We must be trained if we are to function productively in the world as it is today and will be tomorrow. This is as true for Board members as for anyone else. When Board members are trained, it is reasonable and logical to assume that they will be more comfortable and competent in the performance of their important duties. It is, therefore, not surprising to find that an important development in community-serving organizations in recent years has been the emergence of planned programs of Board member education. In many agencies, Jewish and non-Jewish, we find outstanding examples of institutes, seminars, short courses, and conferences devoted to helping Board members learn how to do their jobs more effectively. It is also gratifying to learn that alert and far-sighted professionals and Board members in some of our congregations are aware of this trend and are taking steps to provide regular, systematic, and continuous training as a means of developing effective Boards.

The Role of the Nominating Committee

The Nominating Committee occupies a central place in the process of developing an effective Board. It serves, in a sense, as a Personnel Committee for the Board's own membership. It is responsible for locating, deciding upon, and securing the consent of persons who are to serve on the Board. Its decisions determine to a great extent the leadership of the synagogue in the years ahead. It is, therefore, both an honor and a grave responsibility to be chosen to work on the Nominating Committee.

In view of the important task of the Nominating Committee,

it is recommended that this committee consist of members of the congregation as well as the Board and that it function on a year-round basis, rather than meeting just before the election. For methods of selecting the Nominating Committee, see Chapter V.

Rotation in Office

Limited tenure for Board members has become the accepted practice in almost all congregations. In many, Board members are elected for three-year terms, and the terms are staggered so that one-third of the Board's membership completes its term each year. After a Board member has served two terms comprising six years, he is not eligible for reelection to the Board. A lapse of one year is usually required before such a member is again eligible for nomination as a member of the Board. This practice of rotation and limited tenure has the following advantages:

1. It provides a systematic way of bringing new people to the Board. With new people come new ideas, new points of view, and new skills.

2. It broadens the base of membership interest, understanding, and support.

3. It keeps the lay leadership from becoming ingrown, possessive, and self-perpetuating.

4. It provides for an automatic way of separating non-productive members from the Board.

For the interested and useful Board member whose term has expired, there can be other opportunities for service as a committee member or in special assignments where his experience and knowledge of the synagogue can be helpful. Subsequently, he may, as stated above, be reelected to the Board.

The Board Meeting

The Board of Trustees usually meets once a month. A regular meeting date should be established at the beginning of the congregational season and a schedule of these meetings for the ensuing congregational year should be mailed to each Board member. An agenda should be planned by the president in consultation with the administrator and/or secretary and mailed to all Board members and rabbi prior to the meeting. It is also recommended that the president appoint a parliamentarian at the first meeting of each new congregational year to assist him, whenever required, in the conduct of Board and congregational meetings.

The agenda for Board meetings should contain the following:

1. Opening prayer by the rabbi or a Board member.
2. Approval of minutes of previous meeting.
3. Communications.
4. Report by the president.
5. Monthly financial report by the treasurer.
6. Reports by other officers.
7. Reports of standing committees.
8. Reports by presidents of affiliate organizations.
9. Reports of special committees in order of their appointment.
10. Unfinished business from previous meeting.
11. New business.
12. Comments by the rabbi on the religious program of the congregation as well as discussion of substantive matters pertaining to Judaism and Jewish life in general.

A definite portion of the time of each Board meeting, planned in advance, should be set aside for a spiritual message by the rabbi and for discussion of congregational and general Jewish matters. This will provide an important vehicle for Board member education.

"New business" should not be scheduled on the agenda of the meeting unless a Board member notifies the secretary prior to the meeting. This is being suggested not in the spirit of denying the right of any member to bring up "new business" at a Board meeting but in the interest of *planned* Board meetings and the conservation of time. The president and the secretary usually schedule on the agenda all matters that require the attention of the Board. To surprise the Board with "new business" of which the Board was not apprised prior to the meeting, and for which the members of the Board are not prepared, is not conducive to good meeting procedure.

Minute Book

The Minute Book comprises the official record of the proceedings of the meetings of the Board of Trustees and of the congregation. In it are recorded the policies, the rules and regulations, and the important decisions by which the life of the congregation is governed. From the standpoint of a permanent record, as well as a historical document, the proper keeping of the minutes is most important. The minutes should be kept in a hard cover, standard corporation Minute Book with pre-numbered pages. They should be typewritten on both sides of the page and double spaced. Each page must be accounted for.

The Minutes should contain an accurate, concise account of all proceedings. Generally the arguments on particular questions and the discussion that takes place at the meeting are not made part of the record, and only the final decisions are recorded. The minutes are a record of what is done and not of what is said. Comments made by the rabbi at the Board meeting and discussions on substantive matters should, however, be summarized.

Since the by-laws of most congregations provide that the Board of Trustees must pass upon all membership matters, and in view of the fact that the professional auditors of the congregation's financial records look to the Board minutes for authority on any changes reflected in the account of a member, it is important that the minutes reflect accurately this information. The following suggested arrangement will be helpful:

To Accept New Members

NAME: _____

ANNUAL DUES: $ _____

MEMBERSIHP TO BEGIN: _____

To Accept Increases in Dues

NAME:

FROM: $ _____

TO: $ _____

AS OF: _____

To Transfer from Complimentary to Paying List

NAME: _____

ANNUAL DUES: $ _____

EFFECTIVE AS OF: _____

To Accept Resignations

NAME: _____

EFFECTIVE AS OF: _____

BALANCE OWING: $ _____

REASON FOR RESIGNATION: _____

To Grant Reductions in Dues

NAME: _____

FROM: $ _____

TO: $ _____

EFFECTIVE AS OF: _____

REASON FOR REDUCTION: _____

To Place on Complimentary List

NAME: _____

FOR PERIOD OF: _____

BALANCE OWING: $ _____

DISPOSITION OF SAME: _____

Deaths (Membership Not Replaced)

NAME: _____

BALANCE OWING: $ _____

DISPOSITION OF SAME: _____

To Send First Notice of Suspension

NAME: _____

ANNUAL DUES: $ _____

BALANCE OWING: $ _____

To Suspend from Membership

NAME: _____

BALANCE OWING: $ _____

DISPOSITION OF SAME: _____

The minutes should be carefully indexed so that any matter which has been passed upon at a formal meeting, however remote in time, may be referred to easily and quickly. Card indexes arranged according to subjects taken from the minute captions and a reference to the minute page on which the matter appears will serve the purpose very well.

REFERENCES

FEDER, MAX, *Congregational Boards and Committees,* Synagogue Research Survey #3, NATA-UAHC, 1956.

GWYNN, PRICE H., JR., *Leadership Education in the Local Church,* Westminster Press, 1952.

HANCHETTE, HELEN W., *The Executive and the Board, Some Dynamics of Social Agency Administration,* Family Service Association of America.

HOULE, CYRIL O., *The Effective Board,* Association Press, 1960.

KATZ, IRVING I., *Major Aspects of Synagogue Administration,* UAHC, 1959.

ROUTZANN, MARY SWAIN, *Better Board Meetings,* National Publicity Council for Health and Welfare Services, 1952.

Training Group Leaders, Adult Education Association of the U.S.A., 1956.

Working with Volunteers, Adult Education Association of the U.S.A., 1956.

V Committee
Structure
and Function

WHILE THE BOARD OF TRUSTEES IS INVESTED WITH ADMINISTRATIVE authority, the preliminaries and details of its many important functions and tasks are entrusted to the standing committees as prescribed in the constitution and by-laws, leaving the final policy decisions to the Board.

Committees are the working centers in a congregation. Committees are voluntary work groups in which members of the congregation pursue a course of collective thinking toward creative action on behalf of the total program of the congregation. Well selected committees, carefully organized and thoughtfully guided, are basic to the successful existence and progress of a congregation.

Objectives of the Committee System

The objectives of the committee system in a congregation are:

1. To provide an opportunity for members to serve the synagogue, and thus to widen the base of membership participation.

2. To provide a medium for creative discussion.

3. To utilize special knowledge and experience of members for special tasks.

4. To create a closer understanding on the part of the individual member of the aims, accomplishments, and problems of the synagogue.

5. To expedite the work of the Board by eliminating routine committee matters from being considered at Board meetings.

6. To provide a training-ground for members for future service on the Board.

7. To prevent centralization of the affairs of the congregation in the hands of a few persons.

Principles of Effective Committee Work

Congregational committees do their work most effectively

1. when they have a clear statement and a clear understanding of their purpose;

2. when they have responsible, constructive, and creative chairmen, preferably Board members, who give continuous guidance to the committee process;

3. when the personnel of each committee are members who are interested and qualified;

4. when they meet regularly and prepare carefully the agenda for each meeting;

5. when they have a good meeting place and develop an atmosphere of freedom and congeniality;

6. when they always begin by asking, "What are the pertinent facts related to our assignment?";

7. when they release and utilize the contributions of members who participate actively in discussion, deliberations, and decision-making;

8. when they do their work according to mutually agreed upon rules, and function as a team rather than as individual performers;

9. when they move through their work assignment in an orderly and progressive manner, taking one step at a time;

10. when they develop a good sense of time and timing, and function realistically in relation to time needs and demands;

11. when they keep adequate minutes which are used in preparing reports for presentation to the Board;

12. when they look at themselves from time to time and endeavor to improve upon their work by means of systematic evaluation;

13. when they provide for their members the basic human satisfactions which come when work is well done;

14. when they are guided in their work by a belief in and respect for democratic values;

15. when they are motivated in their work by an appreciation of the purposes and aims of the synagogue and of the high ideals and goals which the synagogue is striving to reach.

The Committee Chairman

Every congregation aspires to secure capable and intelligent lay leaders. The officers are important, of course, to the success of the congregation, but equally significant is the role of the committee chairmen. They seldom get the publicity that is accorded to the "top brass," but they certainly are the key to organizational success.

What kind of a person makes a good chairman? What are the qualifications we seek when we set about to select and appoint these key workers?

If you are a member of a committee and have had a satisfying and productive series of meetings from which you have received a sense of accomplishment, the chances are that you have had a good chairman, and that he worked in a systematic way. The effective chairman conducts himself at meetings along such lines as these:

1. He will be an encouraging person who makes it easy for people to express themselves.

2. He will be a positive person who avoids rejecting or running down the contributions of others.

3. He will be a questioning person who asks for and solicits opinions from all who are there.

4. He will spend time posing, defining, and redefining the problem to help people know precisely what is the point of discussion.

5. He will help the group to define its position at a given time and will constantly seek to summarize the areas of agreement so that the group can move on.

6. He will give good direction to the meeting and will show evidence of having a planful approach.

7. He will inspire confidence because of his sincere interest in the work of the committee and because of his warm regard for the ability of his committee members.

Committee Procedure

1. The president shall appoint the chairmen of all committees and, in consultation with each chairman, shall select the members of his committee.

2. All appointed committees should be charged with their responsibilities and authority in writing.

3. Wherever possible, the president should choose members of the Board of Trustees to chair committees.

4. Representation should be afforded to the affiliate organizations on relevant committees.

5. At its first meeting each committee will determine its regular meeting dates for the year. It is to be remembered that the president (or his designee) is an ex-officio member of all committees and is to be notified of the call for or cancellation of a meeting.

6. No committee is autonomous. Each committee is to recommend all matters of policy for the Board's approval.

7. The recommendations of any committee must be by a majority of its members. Upon a specific request, minority reports may also be submitted.

8. Officers who have the responsibility for the progress of certain committees will contact their chairmen before each Board meeting to ascertain in advance if they have a report. He will make sure that any recommendation to the Board by a committee will be presented at the end of a report in the form of a motion.

9. When the report of a committee meeting is presented to the Board, the report should be in writing and should include a statement of the place and time of the meeting and the attendance. This written report is to become part of the Board minutes.

10. It is imperative that the synagogue office be notified in advance of the call of a committee or subcommittee meeting not already on the calendar, or the cancellation of a meeting.

Areas of Committee Service

As many committees as can function successfully in each area of the synagogue program should be appointed to meet regularly for discussion and planning of departmental projects. In order to give every member of the congregation an opportunity to serve on the committee of his or her choice, it is good practice for the president to send out a letter of invitation to each member to seek participation in committee work, accompanied by a listing of the various committees and a brief description of their functions.

Committees are the key to organizational effectiveness. Congregations which function well and carry forward a good program inevitably have a strong set of committees, with well-defined duties, to serve as many of the following areas of congregational management and activity as is required:

A. FISCAL AND MEMBERSHIP MATTERS

1. *Budget and Finance Committee*
   a. To prepare the annual congregational budget.
   b. To submit the budget to the Board of Trustees for approval and then to the members of the congregation at the annual meeting for their approval.
   c. To supervise the congregational budget.
   d. To render monthly financial statements to the Board of Trustees, through the treasurer.
   e. To review annually the auditor's financial report.
   f. To act on requests for reductions in dues from members of the congregation.
   g. To deal with delinquent members.
   h. To review periodically the dues structure of the congregation.
   i. To review any extra-budgetary expenses for presentation to the Board.
   j. To develop new sources of income.
   k. To study and recommend to the Board constructive financial procedures and policies.
   l. To see to it that the congregation derives an adequate income from *dues* to cover the operating budget.
2. *Bequests and Capital Gifts Committee (or Long-Range Financial Planning Committee)*
   a. To stimulate bequests to the synagogue.
   b. To encourage members of the congregation to take out insurance policies, designating the synagogue as beneficiary.
   c. To stimulate contributions of stocks and bonds where tax situation is advantageous to the donor.

d. To explore the possibility of having members give stock interests or outright interests in their business concerns.

e. To stimulate the establishment of endowment or trust funds.

f. To stimulate the assignment to the synagogue of parcels of property owned by members, the current income going to the congregation.

g. To explore the possibility of becoming yearly beneficiaries from personal and business foundations.

h. To stimulate outright grants.

i. To stimulate outright substantial contributions by members over and above the annual dues.

j. To prepare an attractive brochure on the needs of your congregation and to place it in the hands of members who discuss wills with their clients and have access to people of means.

3. *Tribute Funds Committee*

To stimulate members of the congregation to contribute to special-purpose funds such as the Joy-Sharing and Memorial Funds.

4. *Committee to Maintain National Institutions*

a. To see to it that the national institutions with which the congregation is affiliated and its theological seminary are generously supported by the synagogue through the prescribed national dues and additional voluntary contributions by individuals.

b. To publicize effectively the work of these national institutions to the membership.

c. To act as a liaison committee between the synagogue and the national organizations.

5. *Membership Committee*

a. New Members Subcommittee:

— To send out annually, in the month of August, a letter to the members of the congregation asking them to submit to the synagogue the names of interested prospective members.

— To be on the look-out for newcomers to the community, and to interest friends and relatives who are unaffiliated with any congregation.

— To interview all prospective members.

— To recommend applications of new members to the Board of Trustees.

— To arrange a New Members' Night at the Friday evening services shortly after the opening of the late Friday evening services season.

—To arrange small group gatherings of new members for the purpose of orientation and sociability.

b. Conservation Subcommittee:

To contact all members who submit resignations to the synagogue in an effort to retain their membership.

c. Integration Subcommittee:

— To be in contact with all members on a personal basis and to see to it that they are brought to synagogue functions and are otherwise integrated into the congregation.

— To search out likely candidates from the membership to serve on synagogue committees and in other capacities. The committee shall evaluate talents, abilities, and interests of members, and accordingly make recommendations to the president.

— This subcommittee shall be in charge of all synagogue socials, such as dinners with the rabbi, president, and other officers, and the annual dinner meeting.

— To act as a fellowship or hospitality committee at all social functions of the congregation, and especially at the services on Friday nights.

— This subcommittee shall evaluate instances of exceptional service to the congregation on the part of groups and individuals, and recommend to the Board means of recognition.

—This subcommittee shall be responsible for the creation of new activities which will further foster fellowship in the congregation.

— This subcommittee shall recommend to the Board any new categories of membership in the congregation.

—If possible, this subcommittee shall visit the sick and the bereaved.

B. PHYSICAL PLANT

1. *House Committee*

a. The committee should formulate rules and regulations for the use of synagogue facilities.

b. A schedule of contributions should be set up by the committee and an application for the use of synagogue facilities should be prepared.

c. An inventory should be taken of the physical properties of the synagogue and this record be kept up to date.

2. *Insurance Committee*

This committee should review at least once every two years the insurance portfolio of the congregation.

C. EDUCATIONAL ACTIVITIES

1. *Religious School Committee*

It should be the duty of the Religious School Committee, in cooperation with the rabbi and the educational director, to formulate all regulations necessary for the government of the school, including employment of teachers and adoption of a course of study.

a. This committee should determine the larger principles and policies under which the school shall operate.

b. To see that the school budget is adequate to maintain a good school, and to check that all expenditures are within the established budget.

c. To determine the regulations relative to registration and to assist with registration.

d. To assist with the distribution of school supplies to the children at the beginning of the school year.

e. This committee should determine salary scales, increments, etc.

f. To ratify all major changes in policies of the school.

g. To approve the curriculum presented by the rabbi and the educational director.

h. To confirm all appointments and dismissals of teachers, supervisors, and other school personnel on the recommendations of the rabbi and educational director.

i. To recommend policies relating to Bar/Bas Mitzvah, Confirmation, and high school graduation.

j. To recommend policy with regard to the admission of non-members' children.

k. To suggest all changes in religious school registration fees.

l. To approve the religious school calendar as submitted by the rabbi and educational director.

m. This committee shall cooperate with the parent-teacher's organization in the following areas:

— In creating a Jewish atmosphere in the homes of the children.

— In the celebration of all Jewish holidays, both in the home and in the school.

— To aid the school by assisting in the problems of attendance, transportation, etc.

— Discuss problems relating to the good and welfare of the school. All recommendations are to be submitted to the rabbi, the educational director, and to the Religious School Committee.

— To plan entertainment for the children, such as parties, picnics, etc.

— To encourage and stimulate better social relations between the children as a group and the parents as individuals.

— To conduct P.T.A. meetings throughout the school year and to keep parents informed of the progress of their children in the school.

— To cooperate with the rabbi in all ways possible in the matter of children's services.

2. *Adult Education Committee*

To plan with the rabbi and educational director the program of adult Jewish education in the congregation, such as an institute of Jewish studies, breakfast club and discussion group, Bible class, home study groups, visiting lecturers, courses in Hebrew, etc.

3. *Nursery School Committee*

The duties of this committee are similar to that of the Religious School Committee as given in C. 1.

4. *Library Committee*

To create a synagogue library and establish rules, regulations, and procedures in regard to its physical facilities and operation.

a. To stimulate the interest of members and their children in the reading of Jewish books, and to promote a wider circulation of books from the synagogue library.

b. To plan special exhibits during Jewish Book Month, Jewish Book Week, Religious Book Week, etc.

c. To arrange exhibits on special Jewish occasions.

d. To publicize effectively the library.

e. To stimulate gifts to the synagogue Library Fund.

D. RELIGIOUS ACTIVITIES

1. *Choir Committee*

a. To assist the music director in the selection of choir personnel.

b. To arrange with the music director, in consultation with the rabbi, the best possible liturgical music for the services on the High Holy Days and major festivals, Friday evenings, Saturday mornings, Confirmation, etc.

c. To arrange with the music director, in consultation with the rabbi, the training of children's choirs for participation in Sabbath and festival services.

d. To discuss with the rabbi and the music director the advisability of organizing adult voluntary choirs or glee clubs from among the members of the Sisterhood, Men's Club, Youth Groups, etc.

e. To arrange a music festival during Jewish Music Month.

f. To encourage congregational singing at all services.

2. *Religious Practices or Ritual Committee*

This committee shall work with the rabbi on any innovations deemed necessary in the present religious practices of the congregation, and shall submit for approval any of its recommendations to the Board and to the members of the congregation. It shall also recommend special services for significant congregational observances.

3. *Attendance at Worship Committee*

This committee shall devise ways and means, in consultation with the rabbi, of stimulating attendance at worship services. It shall arrange for the selection of hostesses at the Friday evening social hour, and of those who are to pronounce the blessing over the candles at the service.

4. *Holiday and Special Events Committee*

a. To arrange an annual Chanuko dance and Congregational Seder.

b. Printing of the High Holy Day tickets.

c. The preparation of a High Holy Day folder, and an Annual Memorial Booklet, together with all publicity relating thereto.

d. This committee shall be in charge of all publicity regarding the High Holy Days, in coordination with the Publicity and Public Relations Committee.

e. To make all arrangements for the ceremony of Confirmation, in cooperation with the chairman of the Religious School Committee, the P.T.A., and the Committee of Parents of the Candidates for Confirmation.

f. To be in charge of the annual and special meetings of the congregation.

5. *Religious Retreat Committee*

This committee shall plan and arrange all religious retreats during the year for members, auxiliaries, as well as the Board of Trustees.

6. *Ushers' Committee*

This committee shall be in charge of ushering at all synagogue services and all other congregational functions.

7. *Cemetery Committee*

a. This committee shall determine the need for congregational burial ground.

b. When the need is established, the committee shall ascertain all pertinent facts relative to its acquisition.

c. It shall prepare and recommend to the Board the adoption of by-laws as well as rules and regulations for the cemetery's operation, to be approved at a meeting of the members of the congregation.

d. It shall adopt, subject to Board approval, price schedules and maintenance procedures for the cemetery.

e. It shall recommend the engagement of necessary personnel for the cemetery.

f. It shall conduct a year-round educational program to encourage purchase of pre-need burial plots.

E. PROGRAM, PUBLICITY, AND PUBLIC RELATIONS

1. *Intra-Synagogue Program Coordinating Committee*

This committee shall consist of the rabbi, the administrator, the presidents, and the vice-presidents of the congregation and affiliate organizations, and the program chairmen of all synagogue affiliates. It shall meet during the summer to evaluate the program of the past year, and to plan and coordinate the entire synagogue program for the coming year. This basic calendar of events shall be mimeographed and mailed to the rabbi, officers, and trustees of the synagogue and affiliate organizations, and chairmen of all committees.

2. *Publicity and Public Relations Committee*

a. This committee shall coordinate the publicity material of organizations associated with the congregation.

b. It shall arrange to publish a synagogue bulletin and issue periodic releases to the Jewish and general press.

c. It shall arrange for the publication of the Annual Congregational Report to be mailed to the membership.

d. It shall investigate the possibility of regular or periodic TV and radio programs.

e. It shall review all form letters which are sent by the synagogue to members of the congregation to insure their clarity and effectiveness with reference to the subject with which they are concerned.

f. This committee shall be responsible for the maintenance of a bulletin board and a staff directory in the synagogue.

F. PERSONNEL

1. *Personnel Policy Committee*

a. To gather information from the business world and religious, charitable, and social welfare organizations on current personnel practices and policies.

b. To compile a complete record of information on each staff member.

c. To set a policy on vacations for the synagogue staff.

d. To establish a policy on sick leave.

e. To formulate a program to provide the staff with proper protection against major health and accident hazards as well as adequate retirement pensions. Also to provide benefits for the survivors of staff members who have been in the employ of the synagogue for a long time.

f. To establish a policy of financial assistance to synagogue employees in cases of emergency.

2. *Rabbinical Liaison Committee*

This committee shall consist of the president and vice-presidents of the congregation. The function of this committee is to meet with the rabbi on personal matters and on matters of salary increments, tenure, etc.

G. AUXILIARY ORGANIZATIONS AND DEPARTMENTS

1. *Youth Activities Committee*

The function of this committee is to maintain and promote a program for the youth in the synagogue.

2. *Affiliate Organizations Committee*

The function of this committee is to serve as a liaison between the synagogue and the Sisterhood, Men's Club, Couples' Club, and any other auxiliary organizations of the congregation.

H. LOCAL, REGIONAL, AND NATIONAL COMMUNITY RELATIONS

1. *Social Action Committee*

This committee shall analyze all issues and problems facing the community and the nation in relation to the principles of Judaism, and by the process of education, sensitize the membership to its moral implications. It shall cooperate with the national commission of its national religious body. Members of this committee should serve as representatives of their synagogue to the local Jewish Community Council.

2. *Committee on Cooperation with Other Synagogues*

The function of this committee is to work on matters of mutual interest with other congregations of the community and region.

I. GENERAL ADMINISTRATION, ETC.

1. *Executive Committee*

a. To consider matters which require attention between meetings of the Board of Trustees and submit recommendations concerning the same for action at the regular or special meeting of the Board.

b. To consider such matters as the president or the Board of Trustees may from time to time designate, and to recommend appropriate action to the president or the Board of Trustees concerning the same.

2. *Nominating Committee*

The function of this committee is generally defined in the constitution and by-laws.

3. *Legal Advisory and By-Laws Committee*

a. To take care of all legal matters pertaining to the congregation.

b. To review periodically the by-laws of the congregation and to recommend such changes as are deemed advisable in keeping with new trends in Judaism and new trends in synagogue administration.

c. To prepare a form of bequest to be inserted in the bulletin of the synagogue and in the annual report.

d. To advise the president or presiding chairman on matters of parliamentary law at meetings.

e. To keep the secretary alerted about formal notices that have to be sent out in accordance with legal requirements in regard to the annual meeting of the congregation, special meetings, etc.

4. *Office Administration Committee*

a. To define the duties of the office staff.

b. To recommend the acquisition of such equipment as is necessary to efficiently carry out the work of the office.

5. *Archives Committee*

To gather and maintain all records and reports on the growth and progress of the synagogue so that a complete and thorough historical record will at all times be available.

For more efficient coordination and follow-up, some of our large congregations divide their committee structure into groups, assigning each group of committees to the general direction of one of the officers, as illustrated in the organizational chart in Chapter II.

REFERENCES

Better Boards and Committees, Adult Education Association of U.S.A., 1957.

FRIEDMAN, ALFRED H., and VORSPAN, ALBERT, *The Congregational Social Action Committee,* UAHC, 1958.

KRANTZLER, HAROLD I., *Your Congregation's Adult Jewish Education Committee: A Manual,* UAHC, 1962.

MILLGRAM, A. E., *Handbook for the Congregational School Board Member,* United Synagogue of America, 1953.

RABINOWITZ, BENJAMIN, *Board of Directors, Committees and Their Responsibilities,* National Jewish Welfare Board, 1957.

SCHMIDT, WILLIAM D., *The Executive and the Board in Social Welfare,* Howard Allen, Inc., 1959.

SILLS, DAVID L., *The Volunteers,* Free Press, 1957.

TRECKER, AUDREY R., and HARLEIGH, B., *Committee Common Sense,* William Morrow & Co., 1954.

VORSPAN, ALBERT, and LIPMAN, EUGENE J., *Justice and Judaism,* UAHC, 1956.

VI Financial Management –
Current Needs

MODERN BUSINESSLIKE HANDLING OF SYNAGOGUE FINANCES CALLS FOR careful and systematic budgeting. A budget is the instrument by which we control the financial management of the congregation — "control" in the sense not of curtailment or of keeping costs within narrow limits, but control with a view to applying dependable income to the best advantage, in accordance with need and in keeping with the responsibility for current and future development.

The standard of measurement for congregational cost should be based not on a minimum of satisfaction, not on economy at the expense of program, but on a vital and comprehensive program touching every phase of Jewish life and calculated to satisfy the vital spiritual, educational, and social needs of the membership. Requirements in personnel and services must be carefully weighed and an alert Board of Trustees, Budget and Finance Committee, and membership assure that these needs will be met.

While most of our congregations have recognized the value of this kind of planning, the budget in many instances still does not present a well thought out financial program. Sometimes the budget is a mere listing of unconnected items which fails to show the proper coordination and classification of activities and the relative cost of each division in proportion to the other divisions and to the total expenditures. An ideal budget constitutes a thorough analysis of present need combined with an intelligent forecasting of legitimate future progress. These two together constitute the planning and foresight that make for successful budgeting.

Budget Preparation

A plan for supervising the expenditures and collecting the income of the congregation should be developed on either a fiscal- or calendar-year basis. Before the budget system can be properly adopted, the right basis therefor must be established. Large congregations should be departmentalized along units of activity and an accurate charting of accounts should be set up around which to build the budget procedure. In smaller congregations, where departmental operation is not customary, the chart of accounts should be constructed on the basis of service and object of expenditure.

It is important that expenditures be limited to the income that may, with a reasonable degree of certainty, be expected to be received within the year.

The budget should be a complete financial forecast based on available data, which, in part, should be obtained from the results recorded in prior years. But financial forecasting also requires that the congregation predetermine its future policies and the program of work to be accomplished. Therefore, in formulating a plan for an ensuing accounting year, the following factors must be carefully considered:

1. Extent and intensity of congregational program.
2. The estimated expenditures or costs.
3. The probable income.

A classification of expenditures by departments or units of activity should first be made, detailing the estimates of the expenses necessary to carry out the program of activity for the budget period. The expense budget should include all items that may be reasonably anticipated and should always be a complete statement of operating costs.

After a forecast of the expenses, consideration should next be directed to the possible income that may be made available during the period. The income estimate should be an accurate forecast, conservative, and sure of realization. If there is doubt as to certain income being secured, it should not be included in the estimates.

Servicing of mortgage indebtedness (principal and interest) and the installation of new or additional equipment for the building should not be included as part of the operating budget. Although many congregations carry interest as an operation expense, it is recommended that all items of a capital nature be excluded from the operating budget. These expenditures should be met by pledges to the Building Fund, special campaigns, and assessments.

Assembling the Data

After the expense and income budgets have been compiled and checked, the data should be coordinated and assembled in statement form, in order that the budget may be presented as a comprehensive whole. This presentation should be in such form as will readily display and compare all factors that enter into the budget as reflected in the various calculations. Budget forms utilized by small, medium, and large congregations are shown at the end of the chapter.

Departmental budgets should be approved by the various committees (in consultation with professional heads where such are available) and the budget in its entirety should be reviewed by the Budget and Finance Committee. This should be preceded, for the guidance of the Budget and Finance Committee, by a preliminary meeting of the Board of Trustees for the purpose of discussing the status of the congregation from the standpoint of aims and current program and with improvement and new plans for upbuilding in mind.

After approval of the budget by the Budget and Finance Committee and the Board of Trustees, the budget should be sent to the membership by mail, well in advance of the annual meeting. A better acquaintance with the vital needs which the synagogue is prepared to fill and the wide range of its activities, together with detailed knowledge of what it will cost, makes for greater cooperation and a correspondingly stabilized income.

Application of the Budget

When the budget is formally adopted by the membership at the annual meeting, it becomes the financial guide for the ensuing year. Each division of activity is expected to operate within the approved budget for the year, on a line-by-line basis.

However, a certain amount of flexibility should be allowed in this connection. It is generally considered satisfactory budget practice to permit the overspending of individual budget estimates within a project, provided the total authorized therefor is not exceeded. It might be well to mention here that the flexibility just mentioned is subject to an exception, and this relates to the matter of salaries.

The budget procedure should contain provisions for essential budget transfers or adjustments whenever they appear necessary. These should be accomplished by application to the Budget and Finance Committee or to the Board of Trustees.

To insure conformity with its provisions, a check-up on the budget should be provided through a monthly report of income and expenditures to the Board of Trustees, comparing actual and budget figures for the month and for the year to date.

The synagogue budget fulfils its functions when:

1. It is the result of a thorough thinking through of congregational policy and program.

2. It is arranged according to projects, indicating at a glance the planned divisions of activity and making possible an analysis of proportionate and relative costs.

3. It is a balanced budget, closely conformable to available income.

4. It is strictly adhered to, barring an unforeseen crisis.

5. It embodies, as far as possible, the forecasting of a long-range program.

6. It includes consideration of reserves for emergencies and expansion.

7. Its conclusions are made known to every member of the synagogue in advance and it is approved at the annual congregational meeting.

Dues — The Life Blood of the Synagogue

Every congregation cherishes the ideal of raising annually its operating income in a successful and dignified manner. While the spiritual objectives are obviously of paramount importance, the assurance of an ample treasury to finance the congregational program and to free the professional staff and lay leaders from the necessity of resorting to financial appeals and makeshifts is devoutly to be desired.

Many of us can remember the old practices used in the synagogue for raising the funds necessary for the payment of salaries and the upkeep of the building. There were no schedules of membership dues; in fact, there was no proper definition of membership. The tin box, or *pushke,* was passed at every service, except on the Sabbath and holidays, and the regular worshipers, through these meager contributions, became the financial supporters of the institution. On those occasions when the Torah was read at services, the *parnoss* (president) and *gabbai* (treasurer), or another lay leader, would glance appraisingly at the assembled congregation to determine who might be the most liberal in *schnodering* (pledging contributions) if called up for an *aliyo* (honor of being called to the Torah). The same kind of speculation governed the distribution of honors and *mitzvos* (good deeds) at other occasions. In many congregations, the income from this source also served in part as "perquisites" for the rabbi, cantor, and *shamosh.*

Seats for the High Holy Days were sold for as much as the traffic would bear. On the first day of Rosh Ha-shono, the pulpit became an auction block, from which the various honors which are distributed during the entire High Holy Day season were "knocked down to the highest bidders." A fervent appeal on Yom Kippur eve, during which the institution was pictured as being on its last financial legs, was the culmination of a series of fundraising measures which provided the synagogue with the major part of its income for the entire year. The success or failure of the congregation for the ensuing year was determined largely by the income derived from the High Holy Day tickets and appeals.

Fortunately, some early adherents of American Reform Judaism included leaders in commerce, industry, and the professions who realized that a religious institution, although run on a nonprofit basis, had to be conducted in a businesslike manner. The synagogue could not progress without an assured income, a steady and constant dues-paying membership, and a planned program of expenditures. Existing methods of fund-raising were examined, the most objectionable were discarded, others changed to conform to the dignity of a place of worship, and those which provided an assured income were retained. Thus the cheap auctions, the impassioned appeals, the extraordinary deference to the wealthy members of the congregation, and the public announcement of individual gifts have disappeared from the services of many congregations. The pulpit is no longer a market place for the sale of ritual honors, and the synagogue no emporium for the barter of special privileges.

To meet its annual operating budget, the synagogue of today has developed certain regular sources of income. The major source of income in most congregations is from dues, i.e., definite annual contributions by the members. Dues occupy a foremost place in the economy of the synagogue, and they have been rightly designated as the lifeblood and the backbone of congregational financing.

Surveys conducted in recent years reveal the fact that there has been a growing trend in our congregations to meet their operating budgets largely or exclusively through income from dues. More and more of our congregational lay leaders are coming to realize that dues are the soundest, most dignified, and most dependable source of congregational income. A substantial income from dues enables the professional staff and lay leaders of the congregation to direct more of their time and energies to the purposes relevant to a synagogue, namely, the study and practice of Judaism, and to the betterment of the congregational program.

A rummage sale is not relevant to Judaism; a bazaar is not relevant to Judaism; an ad journal which takes thousands of man-hours to put together is not relevant to the purposes of a congregation. Constant fund-raising to meet the annual congregational budget not only taxes beyond capacity the energies of the congregation's leadership, at the expense of relevant synagogue programming and the rendering of personal services, but has a demoralizing effect upon the congregants, and places religion on an undignified level.

Congregations where the income from dues covers only a small portion of their operating budget and where year-round fund-

raising is the "order of the day" will do well to reexamine and re-
think their entire financial set-up, giving earnest consideration to
the strengthening of their dues structure, which is the heart of
sound synagogue financing.

How Much Dues Shall a Member Pay?

Any discussion of dues inevitably brings up the oft-asked question, "How much dues shall a member pay?" For many years, it
has been advocated that every congregation should strive to obtain an income from dues which will be sufficient to cover the full
program or operating budget. Using this premise, the formula to
be followed is that *the basic dues in a congregation should be
equal to the per member cost.* In other words, if a congregation
has a membership of 100 and a budget of $25,000, the basic dues
should be $250 per member. Since it is not likely that every mem-
ber or prospective member is financially able to pay $250, a grad-
uated scale should be provided, allowing the member of lesser
means to pay below the basic rate of dues, insisting that the affluent member pay above the basic rate, and striving to have the
majority of the membership pay the basic rate. This is illustrated
in the form on the following page.

Rabbi Harry Essrig of Temple Emanuel, Grand Rapids, Michigan, a congregation which is over a century old, put it this way
in his congregational bulletin:

> Some fundamental changes have occurred in our movement
> concerning the matter of temple finances. The concepts pre-
> vailing in previous generations which have prevented ma-
> ture handling of budgetary techniques will soon be on their
> way out. Too many have regarded their support of the tem-
> ple as a charity obligation or as a responsibility to be shoul-
> dered only by those of exceptional means. Too many have
> believed that in applying modern business techniques to
> the administrative aspects of the congregation we were some-
> how degrading the religious institution. It was not realized
> that this forced us to spend too much time on the problem

TEMPLE BETH SHOLOM ALL INCLUSIVE DUES PLAN

In accordance with Jewish tradition, each member shall, by self-evaluation of his own circumstances and ability to pay, determine the amount of his dues. In order to remain in good standing, he shall notify the treasurer on the form provided to him, by_____ . The amount will be kept confidential.   In determining the amount of his dues, it is recommended that each member be guided by the following schedule:

Income	Dues	Income	Dues
Less than $ 7,500	$150	$16,000 to $18,000	$320 - $360
$ 7,500 to 8,500	$150 - 170	18,000 to 20,000	360 - 400
8,500 to 10,000	170 - 200	20,000 to 25,000	400 - 500
10,000 to 12,000	200 - 240	25,000 to 30,000	500 - 600
12,000 to 14,000	240 - 280	More than 30,000	More than 600
14,000 to 16,000	280 - 320		

However, in no event shall dues be less than $150 per year for a regular membership.   Single membership will be one-half of the appropriate family dues.   The present minimum of young married couples (under 25 years of age) will remain in force.

In addition thereto, there shall be charged and remitted to the Union of American Hebrew Congregations 10% of the dues pledged.

FOR YOUR RECORDS: I have undertaken to pay $_____dues for _____(plus 10% for the Union of American Hebrew Congregations).

Method of payment_____

- -

(DETACH HERE AND MAIL LOWER CARD BY_____)

Having sincerely considered my relationship to Temple Beth Sholom and my own financial ability, I hereby agree to pay:

DUES – – $_____
UAHC DUES (10%) $_____
Total $_____

_____Enclosed please find check for $_____

METHOD OF PAYMENT: ☐ Annual in advance
☐ One-half, August 15th
One-fourth, November 15th
One-fourth, February 15th

Name:_____ Phone_____

Address:_____ Date _____

of balancing the budget at the neglect of the more important spiritual and cultural concerns.

The tendency in the Reform movement today is to expect all the members to recognize fully their obligation for the support of the synagogue. Making it possible for the congregation to exist is as much an obligation as any other which a family incurs in providing for the various needs of the unit. The simplest and most common approach is to think in terms of the per capita cost; that is, to divide the total budget by the number of members. This is a good clue as to what we may expect from the members. In an ideal situation, assuming that all people were of equal economic status, or in the case of a large congregation where this is possible, most everyone would pay the same amount of dues. However, in real life, that is not true. Many families are not capable of meeting the per capita cost and hence the more affluent are expected to give more, as determined by the Finance Committee. This is a good approach because, on the one hand, it establishes the financial responsibility of each member up to his capacity, and on the other, it provides an opportunity for the generous impulse to express itself. Those who have more are willing to make up for those who have to give less. This is a wonderful religious principle and makes good sense as well.

Rabbi Martin E. Katzenstein, associate rabbi of Temple Israel, St. Louis, recommends that the following basic steps be taken:

1. The members appoint a committee to consider the scope of the synagogue's program. Consultation with the Union of American Hebrew Congregations and neighboring congregations of similar definition will provide the information that is required and will give the committee a reliable understanding of the costs of carrying out the program it envisions.

2. The committee reports its findings to the Board of Trustees for consideration and asks the trustees to commit themselves both to the program and to its financing.

3. The trustees then take this program to an open membership meeting in order to get a similar commitment from the membership. The philosophy underlying this presentation is one in which the basic task is the satisfying of need rather than the paring of

program to fit available funds. The question will arise: "How are we going to get the money to finance this program?" The reply will come somewhere in the course of the discussion. Someone will find himself saying publicly, "Either we are a congregation or we aren't. If we are a congregation, then we must refuse to settle for less than a good program of congregational activity."

4. The membership should now be convinced of the need. A second committee reports on the possibilities for growth in the coming year. The membership is asked to do a little mental long division. When one divides the number of members that the congregation anticipates having in the next year into the anticipated cost of operation, one comes up with the average cost of operation per family.

5. Each member is asked to relate his income to the average cost per family. If he considers himself average, he should want to make a contribution to the operation of his congregation that is equal to the average cost per member. If his income is above average, he should adjust his contribution accordingly, and if his income is below average, he should be assured that his contribution, as long as it represents his best thinking on the subject, will be accepted with gratitude.

6. In establishing a dues program such as this, it is assumed by all that every member will contribute to the extent of his ability *in line* with the anticipated expenditure of the congregation. This being the case, *each member can be advised that he will not be asked for any additional contributions for purposes of congregational operation unless he and his fellow members do not assume their fair share of the responsibility.*

A problem that normally reveals itself grows out of the fact that the membership is composed of families who have children in the religious school and others whose children are not of religious school age or who have no children. They will perhaps ask: "Why should we pay to support those who have children in the school?" The answer is a simple one. In the secular community we pay taxes for the support of many facilities that we cannot or do not choose to take advantage of. We do this on the basis of our interest in the total community, and we would not consider asking for special consideration because of our status as non-participants. The Jewish community of the future is going to rest on the shoulders of the young people of today, and if we do not train them adequately, there will be no future for American Judaism. This is a principle that *must* be maintained. If it is modified in any way, the repercussions can extend to other aspects of congregational life. One could logically state that even though he sends his children to the religious school, he has no interest in the worship program of the congregation and thus should be exempted from its financial support. A congregation cannot provide partial services to its members. Both aspects of the definition of a congregation must continually be subscribed to: service to the membership and service to the Jewish community. The maxim in the Sayings of the Fathers applies poignantly here: "Separate thyself *not* from the community."

Supplementary Sources of Income

While dues should be the principal source of income, there are a number of existing regular and special supplementary sources of income utilized in many congregations. Some of these sources are:

1. *Use of Synagogue Facilities*

Congregations derive income from the use of synagogue facilities for weddings, Bar Mitzvahs, social meetings of outside organizations, etc. In this connection, it should be emphasized that the House Committee of the congregation should formulate rules and regulations for the use of the synagogue's facilities which will be in keeping with the dignity and decorum of a house of God and should see to it that these provisions are strictly complied with by those who utilize the synagogue's facilities for various functions.

2. *Cemetery Surplus*

In many congregations the cemetery is a source of considerable revenue. The surplus from cemetery operations may be made available, in whole or in part, to the congregational treasury for current program expenditures or for a stabilizing or reserve fund.

3. *Tribute Funds*

Congregations should stimulate and develop Tribute Funds in the form of In Memoriam and Happy Occasion contributions. These involve free-will gifts, in commemoration of the *yahrzeit* of a relative or friend, or in honor of such happy occasions as births, weddings, Bar Mitzvahs, Confirmations, anniversaries, etc. Some congregations use these gifts for current operating expenses, others for special purposes, such as the purchase of books for the congregational library, purchase of prayer books and hymnals, purchase of special equipment for the religious school, and still other congregations utilize these funds for philanthropic work.

4. *Yahrzeit Memorial Tablet and Memorial Book*

Many congregations derive considerable income from the privilege granted to their members to inscribe the name of a departed one on a Yahrzeit Memorial Tablet, displayed prominently in the synagogue. Names of the deceased are read from the pulpit on the anniversary date and at the Memorial services on Yom Kippur and festivals. The contribution for the establishment of this type of memorial varies from $150 to $500. Individuals frequently purchase name plates not only for their departed relatives but make a reservation for themselves.

Some congregations have, in addition, instituted the Memorial Book or Golden Book, requesting a fixed amount of $25 to $250 per page for a memorial inscription. Having a Memorial Tablet and a Memorial Book affords the members an opportunity to select the memorial best suited to their tastes.

5. *Memorial Booklet*

In many congregations special memorial contributions are made in connection with the printing of names of members and relatives in a special Memorial Booklet distributed at the Yom Kippur Memorial service.

6. *Book of Life*

A number of congregations have in recent years instituted a Book of Life to enable members to commemorate important happy events in their lives, such as weddings, births, Bar and Bas Mitzvahs, and Confirmations.

There are many forms of fund-raising being utilized by congregations. However, as stated previously, it is not germane to the purpose of the synagogue to engage in continuous fund-raising. *The means of securing adequate budgetary income is in the direction of larger support from membership dues, the soundest, most dignified, and most dependable source of synagogue income.* The trend is away from fund-raising by means of bazaars and entertainment, sporadic drives for donations, or special appeals from the pulpit.

REFERENCES

CASHMAN, ROBERT E., *Finances of a Church*, Harper & Bros., 1949.

CROSSLAND, WELDON, *How to Increase Church Income*, Abingdon-Cokesbury Press, 1947.

FEDER, MAX, *Congregational Budgets and Membership Income*, Synagogue Research Survey #1, NATA-UAHC, 1956.

———— *Temple Finances and Membership Income*, Synagogue Research Survey #6, NATA-UAHC, 1961.

———— *The Synagogue and Finances*, UAHC, 1959

HOLT, DAVID R., II, *Handbook of Church Finance*, Macmillan Co., 1960.

JOHNSON, ERNEST F., and ACKERMAN, EMORY J., *The Church as Employer, Money Raiser and Investor*, Harper & Bros., 1959.

PENDLETON, OTHNIEL, JR., *New Techniques for Church Fund Raising*, McGraw-Hill Book Co., 1955.

SCHOEN, MYRON E., "Financing the Congregation Through Adequate Dues," *National Jewish Post and Opinion*, July, 1960.

SCHWARZ, JACOB D., *The ABC of Synagogue Financing*, UAHC, 1952.

BUDGET PRESENTATION FOR LARGER CONGREGATION

Symbols

s — Sisterhood   m — Men's Club   b — Building Fund
nf — Originally budgeted but eliminated because of lack of funds
c — Contributions, miscellaneous   gf — General Fund

Programming	1957 Budget	1957 Other Sources	Projected 1958 Budget	Approved 1958 Budget
1. RELIGIOUS SCHOOL	- -	- -		
Salaries: Teachers		- -	- -	
			- -	
Principal	- -		- -	
Director of Educational Programming	- -		- -	
Secretaries	- -		- -	
Library: Book processing	- -		- -	
Books for teachers	- -		- -	
Books for adults and pupils		- -	- -	
		- -	- -	
		- -	- -	
Essential library equipment	- -		- -	
Holiday celebrations, assemblies		- -	- -	
Scholarships for needy children	- -		- -	
Textbooks for scholarships		- -	- -	
Youth Conclave in 1958		- -	- -	
Youth and Joy Club Advisors		- -	- -	
Scout troop expenses		- -	- -	- -
Camp scholarships		- -	- -	
2. ADULT ACTIVITIES AND PROGRAMS	- -			
Adult Education Committee	- -		- -	
Membership Committee	- -		- -	
Social Action Committee			- -	
Institute on Judaism		- -	- -	
Programs, Printing, etc.			- -	- -
3. SANCTUARY NEEDS	- -			
Choir music	- -		- -	
Shovuos service program	- -		- -	
Candles and Oneg Shabbat linen	- -	- -	- -	
Gifts to Bar Mitzvahs				
Prayer book, Kiddush cup, or candlesticks	- -	- -		
		- -	- -	- -
4. HIGH HOLY DAY ARRANGEMENTS	- -			
Rental charge for 425 chairs	- -		- -	
Boutonnières for ushers, participants	- -		- -	
Printing cards of admission	- -		- -	
Supervision of children's services	- -		- -	
Miscellaneous	- -		- -	- -
5. ORGANIZATIONAL DUES	- -			
Rotary Club — rabbi's dues	- -			
National Assoc. of Temple Administrators	- -			
National Assoc. of Temple Educators			- -	- -

BUDGET PRESENTATION FOR LARGER CONGREGATION (Cont.)

Programming (Continued)	1957 Budget	1957 Other Sources	Projected 1958 Budget	Approved 1958 Budget
6. CONVENTION TRAVEL	— —			
Rabbi's fare to Central Conference of American Rabbis and Western Association of Reform Rabbis	— —		— —	
Fare for delegates to UAHC Biennial in fall of 1958	— —		— —	— —
7. CONTINGENCY	— —			
Non-budgeted items, gifts, unscheduled expenses, etc.	— —		— —	— —
Public Relations				
8. TEMPLE PUBLICATION	— —			
Temple News and postage	— —		— —	
Sabbath service announcements	— —		— —	— —
9. ADVERTISING, SUBSCRIPTIONS	— —			
Arizona Post subscriptions	— —		— —	
Arizona Post: fall advertisements	— —		— —	
High Holy Day broadcast, telephone line, and newspaper ad	— —		— —	
Church display card	— —		7 —	
Daily reporter	— —		— —	
Publicity Brochures			— —	— —
Office Expenses				
10. SUPPLIES AND EQUIPMENT	— —		— —	— —
11. AUDITING	— —		— —	— —
12. SECRETARIAL SALARIES	— —			
Chief office secretary				
Expert in typing, shorthand				
Knowledge of bookkeeping				
Knows temple members, temple patterns, and traditions				
Supervises office routine	— —		— —	
Receptionist and typist, shorthand				
Good technique in receiving and transmitting messages				
Must be familiar with temple routine	— —		— —	
Bookkeeper: (part-time)			— —	
Mimeographer, stencil cutter				
Knowledge of graphic arts (part-time)			— —	— —

BUDGET PRESENTATION FOR LARGER CONGREGATION (Cont.)

Salaries	1957 Budget	1957 Other Sources	Projected 1958 Budget	Approved 1958 Budget
13. RABBI	— —			— —
14. EXECUTIVE DIRECTOR	— —			— —
15. DIRECTOR OF MUSIC	— —		— —	— —
16. MUSIC: Choir and organist	— —			
Choir — 4 voices	— —		— —	
Organist	— —		— —	— —

Fixed Expenses

	1957 Budget	1957 Other Sources	Projected 1958 Budget	Approved 1958 Budget
17. MORTGAGE REDUCTION Annual payment due		— —	— —	— —
18. INTEREST ON MORTGAGE	— —			
		— —	— —	— —
19. LAND PURCHASES Principal and Interest		— —	— —	— —
20. STREET ASSESSMENTS	— —			
1958 — Principal and interest	— —		— —	— —

Balance of principal payments:
Dec., 1959 — — —
Dec., 1960 — — —
Dec., 1961 — — —
Dec., 1962 — — —
Dec., 1963 — — —
Dec., 1964 — — —

	1957 Budget	1957 Other Sources	Projected 1958 Budget	Approved 1958 Budget
21. PENSION: RABBI	— —			
Total pension costs: — —				
Rabbi's portion: — —				
Temple's portion: — —	— —		— —	— —
22. F.I.C.A. All employees, except rabbi	— —		— —	— —

Maintenance

	1957 Budget	1957 Other Sources	Projected 1958 Budget	Approved 1958 Budget
23. BUILDING UPKEEP	— —			
Tools and supplies				
Kitchen equipment, utensils				
Miscellaneous painting				
Heating and cooling systems upkeep				
New power lawn mower			— —	— —
24. LANDSCAPING	— —			
Patio — —				
Grounds — —			— —	

BUDGET PRESENTATION FOR LARGER CONGREGATION (Cont.)

Maintenance (Continued)	1957 Budget	1957 Other Sources	Projected 1958 Budget	Approved 1958 Budget
25. FURNISHING AND REPLACEMENT	– –			
Completion of furnishing of all temple facilities			– –	
26. CARETAKER and SPECIAL HELP	– –			
Permanent couple and residence	– –		– –	
Special help, as needed	– –		– –	– –
27. RABBI'S HOUSE: RENTAL ALLOWANCE	– –		– –	– –
28. RABBI'S AUTO: EXPENSE ALLOWANCE	– –		– –	– –
29. TELEPHONES	– –			
2 trunk lines at monthly	– –			
Toll calls and telegrams	– –		– –	– –
30. UTILITIES	– –		– –	– –
31. INSURANCE	– –			
Total insurance in force				
Public liability – –				
Fidelity bonds – –				
Fire, extra coverage, and vandalism – –				
Workman's compensation – –				
Glass – –				
Prorated annually:			– –	– –

TOTAL BUDGET: – –

ESTIMATE OF MISCELLANEOUS INCOME: – –

AMOUNT TO BE RAISED FROM DUES: – –

1958 BUDGET SUMMARY

	1957 Budget	1957 Other Sources	1957 Total	1958 Budget
Programming				
1. RELIGIOUS SCHOOL	--	--	--	--
2. ADULT ACTIVITIES AND PROGRAMS	--		--	--
3. SANCTUARY NEEDS	--	--	--	--
4. HIGH HOLY DAY ARRANGEMENTS	--		--	--
5. ORGANIZATIONAL DUES	--		--	--
6. CONVENTION TRAVEL	--		--	-=
7. CONTINGENCY	--		--	--
Public Relations				
8. TEMPLE PUBLICATION	--		--	--
9. ADVERTISING, SUBSCRIPTIONS	--		--	--
Office Expenses				
10. SUPPLIES AND EQUIPMENT	--		--	--
11. AUDITING	--		--	--
12. SECRETARIAL SALARIES	--		--	--
Salaries				
13. RABBI	--		--	--
14. EXECUTIVE DIRECTOR	--		--	--
15. DIRECTOR OF MUSIC	--		--	--
16. CHOIR AND ORGANIST	--		--	--
Fixed Expenses:				
17. MORTGAGE REDUCTION		--	--	--
18. INTEREST ON MORTGAGE	--		--	--
19. LAND PURCHASES		--	--	--
20. STREET ASSESSMENTS	--		--	--
21. PENSION: RABBI	--		--	--
22. F.I.C.A.	--		--	--
23. BUILDING UPKEEP	--		--	--
24. LANDSCAPING	--		--	--
25. FURNISHING AND REPLACEMENT	--		--	--
26. CARETAKER AND SPECIAL HELP	--		--	--
27. RABBI'S HOUSE: RENTAL ALLOW.	--		--	--
28. RABBI'S AUTO: EXP. ALLOWANCE	--		--	--
29. TELEPHONES	--		--	--
30. UTILITIES	--		--	--
31. INSURANCE	--		--	--
	--	--	--	--

ESTIMATE OF DUES, MISCELLANEOUS AND POTENTIAL INCOME FOR THE FISCAL YEAR 1958 - 1959

MEMBERSHIP DUES INCOME . . . . $ — — —

TEMPLE SISTERHOOD (See #1)
Our Sisterhood has indicated that it will be able to assist the religious
school budget to the extent of — — — . This amount equals what it is
paying during the current year . . . . $ — — —

TEMPLE MEN'S CLUB (See #1)
The Men's Club contributed — — — for school extension work and
scholarships this year. There is no indication, at present, to what
extent the Men's Club will be able to help financially next year . . . . . . $ — — —

RELIGIOUS SCHOOL TUITIONS (See #1)
Students, under certain conditions, are eligible for tuition rates. A
good average for this source of income would be . . . . $ — — —

CAMP SARATOGA SURPLUS FUND (See #1)
Due to an unexpected surplus last year, there is a credit available
for scholarships to Camp Saratoga this year . . . . $ — — —

TUITION SCHOLARSHIP FUND (See #1)
This fund incorporates the need for full-tuition scholarships and
partial-tuition scholarships.

> FULL-TUITION SCHOLARSHIPS: We have — — — students
> whose parents cannot afford temple membership. They receive
> full-tuition scholarships. At the rate of — — per student
> (estimated cost of carrying a student for one year), the
> scholarships involved a cost of — — .

> PARTIAL-TUITION SCHOLARSHIPS: Approximately — — of
> our students (— —) are children of families unable to pay
> the minimum dues. It is estimated that these — — students
> require a subsidy of approximately — — to meet the costs
> of their training.

> Members are invited to contribute to the Tuition Scholarship
> Fund to help meet this situation.

WEEK-DAY HEBREW CLASSES (See #1)
There is no charge to members for religious school instruction.
However, the possibility has been mentioned that a charge of
about — — might be made for the — — odd students of the
week-day Hebrew department.

LIBRARY BOOKS FOR ADULTS AND STUDENTS (See #1)
There is no budgetary allowance. This need is being met
through individual contributions and the Sisterhood sponsorship
of a Library Tea.

ANNUAL CONTRIBUTORS (NON-MEMBERS)
This category includes annual contributions from families
who are not full-participating members. . . . . $ — — —

MEMORIAL PLAQUES
The sale of Memorial Plaques generally averages — — — .
This source of income might be enlarged through an energetic
campaign . . . . $ — — —

ESTIMATE OF DUES, MISCELLANEOUS AND POTENTIAL INCOME FOR THE FISCAL YEAR 1958 - 1959 (Continued)

YOM KIPPUR REMEMBRANCE BOOK
Our first Remembrance Book produced — —. The second, — —,
after printing costs had been deducted. This income might
level off between — — and — — .... $ — — —

YOM KIPPUR FREE-WILL OFFERING
Last year was the first start of this fund. Receipts totaled
 — —. It is felt that with adequate publicity, this Free-Will
Offering might become a fine source of income .... $ — — —

ANNUAL TEMPLE DINNER-DANCE
This annual event is not a fund-raising dance. With proper
supervision, however, a profit of around — — is possible........... $ — — —

RENTALS
The rental income varies considerably from year to year.
Though we have reached close to — — so far this year, a good
average, unless conditions change drastically, would be .... $ — — —

CONTRIBUTIONS (Miscellaneous Funds)
General contributions to the Remembrance and other funds have
totaled — — for the 9-month period this year. It would be safe
to assume that we will reach — — . (The Remembrance Fund is
earmarked for school [#1] and sanctuary needs [#3].) .... $ — — —

BUILDING FUND (See #17, 18)
There are ample pledges that can be collected to meet the annual
mortgage payments of — — . Should pledge payments slow down
somewhat, new contributions might make up the difference and
help us meet the budgeted amount. .... $ — — —

SPECIFIC ITEM CONTRIBUTIONS (See #25)
There are many items, largely in the category of Furnishing
and Replacements (#25), which cannot be included within the
annual operating budget. A separate listing of these items is
available. Members are encouraged to acquire such articles
or to contribute toward their acquisition. All such items are
acknowledged appropriately and suitably engraved, if possible.

Total Anticipated Income. .... $ — — —

THESE ARE YOUR TEMPLE FUNDS

BUILDING FUND

Ten years of expansion have compelled us to build three temple units – the auditorium, school classrooms and Convocation Building. Meeting the needs of new settlers has necessitated mortgage obligations. The Building Fund provides an excellent depository for cash gifts, pledges, annuities, insurance benefits and bequests. Contributions make possible needed improvements and the purchase of important equipment and furniture. Where possible, such gifts may be inscribed appropriately.

RABBI'S DISCRETIONARY FUND

Within the pastoral activities of our rabbi, there are opportunities, almost daily, when he is called upon to provide money for a needy individual or family. These "last resort" requests cannot be turned over to other agencies, if any immediate help is to be given. With adequate funds, he can bestow these gifts anonymously as well. Contributors can share in this "mitzvah" by large or small contributions, sent directly to the rabbi, or to the temple office.

CAMP FOR LIVING JUDAISM

Reform temples of the western area have joined in the support of a beautiful camp for youth and adults, at Saratoga, California. Already beyond the experimental stage, this 300-acre estate now serves the recreational needs of our youth in a wholesome and edifying atmosphere. Your gift not only helps this great project but also defrays the cost of summer camperships for our temple youth. The major portion of contributions from our religious school students also support the camp scholarships.

REMEMBRANCE FUND

This is our best-known fund. Traditionally, Jews associate the anniversary of the passing of loved ones with acts of kindness and charity. The fund is remembered most frequently at yahrzeit time and in memory of our recently departed. This fund specifically aids devotional and religious school needs and helps create a rich Jewish life.

NATIONAL COMBINED CAMPAIGN

The mother institutions of Liberal Judaism are the Hebrew Union College – Jewish Institute of Religion and the Union of American Hebrew Congregations. Our temple members pay an annual tax to assist these worthy agencies. This self-imposed tax is not adequate, however; hence the need for further voluntary gifts for these founts of Jewish life in America.

TEMPLE BEAUTIFUL FUND

There are countless items in a temple which cannot be purchased from current income. Such gifts beautify the interior and exterior of the building. We have been fortunate in receiving some very fine gifts in honor of Bar Mitzvahs, weddings, and similar joyous occasions. Unless earmarked for a specific item, contributions are placed in a permanent fund and used for the purchase of suitable objects or installations.

SCHOLARSHIP FUND

Our religious school, wholly supported by our Sisterhood, does not turn away any deserving child whose parents are unable to pay the costs of tuition and books. Each scholarship costs $40. Contributions to this fund

help meet the cost of one such scholarship. Names of students benefiting are never revealed, however. Gifts to this fund may also be earmarked for other types of scholarships, if desirable.

LIBRARY FUND

Tucson needs an adequate Jewish Reading and Reference Room. Our ultimate desire is to have an extensive library, serving the needs of our members and the general community. Cultural programs, as part of library extension work, will also be encouraged. Cash gifts may be given directly to the fund, or specific book titles selected. Name plates with the donor's name and the occasion of the gift are inserted in each book.

MEMORIAL PLAQUE FUND

Individual name plaques may be added to our Memorial Tablet in the temple foyer. These Plaques perpetuate the everlastingly the fond memory of our dear ones. Each year, upon the anniversary of the yahrzeit and at all Yizkor services, the light opposite the name is kindled. The cost for each plaque is $110, and members may arrange terms of payment that are most satisfactory.

PRAYER BOOK FUND

Our sabbath prayer books, distributed at services, are often given to memorialize the name of a dear departed one. In frequent cases, books are also given in honor of a happy occasion. Each prayer book has the desired name inscribed in gold letters on the cover, with a suitable name plate mounted inside the cover. Both names and occasions are vividly recalled in moments of prayer and contemplation. The cost of the prayer book and inscription is $3.00.

YOUR TEMPLE IS WORTHY OF YOUR SUPPORT

BUDGET PRESENTATION FOR SMALLER CONGREGATION

In the budget presented herein, you will find a new grouping of items of expenditure. This change has been made so that our budget may reflect more clearly the programs and activities of the temple, and to conform to modern accounting practices. Despite the regrouping, however, the individual items have been altered very slightly. A few items (e.g., Hebrew instruction) appear as both income and expenditure entries; these are self-sustaining, that is, the fees paid by parents for Hebrew instruction for their children are shown as income, and the monies so collected are used to pay the teachers and thus they appear as expenditures.

There are three main groups of entries:

1. Religious Activities
2. Grounds, Buildings, and Equipment
3. Administration and Communications

Some explanatory remarks on these headings may be in order. But you might like to refer first to the illustration of how our budget is to be apportioned. You will see that by far the most important areas are the religious activities and the synagogue in which they are housed.

RELIGIOUS ACTIVITIES

The principal function of the synagogue, we conceive, is to serve as a focal point, a home, and an inspiration to our congregation. Under such a concept it has seemed logical to group together worship services, religious and Hebrew instruction, and the relationship of the synagogue with the larger body of Judaism through its national affiliation and rabbinical conferences.

Thus we find, budgeted under religious activities, such items as the religious school, salaries and fees for our rabbi and for the organists and soloist, High Holy Day costs, the annual dues to the UAHC, and the cost of conference attendance.

A small reduction in the school budget appears to be possible, in the light of our experience in 1959. A new item is the school reference library. In previous years, we used the reference works of the Bureau of Jewish Education as teaching aids for the pupils in the higher grades and as additional sources for the teachers themselves. Following the dissolution of the Bureau, it became apparent that we would have to provide our own resource materials, as without this the children and teachers have no resources available to them. The item in the budget represents a modest beginning for this most important need.

BUILDINGS, GROUNDS, AND EQUIPMENT

This group of items includes the physical properties, the reducing of their indebtedness, routine maintenance, repair, and replacement or additions to furnishings, as well as light and heat, janitor services, and so on. It does not include the Building Fund itself, which is not a part of the yearly budget.

Happily, the reduction in our indebtedness has resulted in a reduction in the interest to be paid in 1960. Aside from this item some increase has to be made for three main reasons. First, the increased use of the synagogue has necessitated more hours of work; i.e., custodian's pay and a greater consumption of janitor's supplies. The 1960 budget shows the need for not only a full-time janitor but scheduled part-time work. Second, some additional schoolroom furniture is needed and window blinds and acoustical tiling are to be programmed, one or two rooms at a time, until completed some years hence. That portion to be done in 1960 is, of course, budgeted under furnishings and replacements. Cost of maintenance is increasing as expected, as our properties slowly age, and shows up under maintenance and supplies. As an example, the gradual deterioration of the brickwork of the synagogue which is overdue for protective treatment to prevent major damage is cited. Third, a small increase results from the direct cost increase that follows the national inflationary trend. It shows up partly in supplies and wages, and partly in taxes and insurance. Insurance is slightly higher since we have chosen to pay premiums by installments to make it easier to meet commitments on time.

ADMINISTRATION AND COMMUNICATIONS

Along with the gratifying increase in synagogue activities goes an enlarged bulletin and more postage. However, the main increase in this group of items comes from the need for essentially a full-time secretary (actually 30 hours per week for 40 weeks). It has become impossible for the synagogue to operate on the present allocated secretarial time. Our programs have expanded with each year and we have not kept pace therewith. We cannot operate a synagogue program without full-time secretarial help. (We have felt this need for some time, but have tried to keep costs down by "getting by" with part-time service. The time has come, at last, when part-time work, however efficient, can no longer do the whole job.) The cost of all these items together has therefore risen by $1125.00. It should be noted that the total administrative cost represents only about 8 per cent of the whole budget.

APPROXIMATE DISTRIBUTION
OF THE
1960 BUDGET

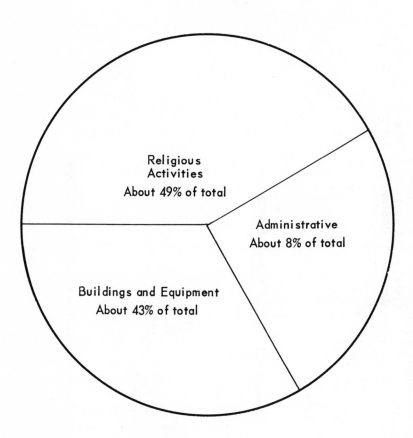

Religious
Activities
About 49% of total

Administrative
About 8% of total

Buildings and Equipment
About 43% of total

RELIGIOUS AND EDUCATIONAL PROGRAM

	1958 Actual	1959 Proposed	1959 Actual	1960 Proposed	1960 Total
1. Religious School					
2. Hebrew School					
3. Library					
4. High Holy Day Music					
5. UAHC Dues					
6. Convention Travel					
7. Rabbi Salary					
8. Pension, Rabbi					
9. Sabbath Music					

BUILDINGS, GROUNDS AND EQUIPMENT

	1958 Actual	1959 Proposed	1959 Actual	1960 Proposed	1960 Total
10. Interest on Mortgage					
Amortization Mortgage and Loan Elmer Ave. }					
11. Maintenance					
12. Supplies for Building					
13. Grounds Maintenance					
14. Furnishing and Replacement					
15. Custodian, Full and Part-Time					
16. Professional Window Washing					
17. Elmer Avenue Residence					
18. Cemetery Caretaker					
19. Cemetery Maintenance and Improvements					
20. Gas and Electricity					
21. Insurance					
22. Water and Sewer Tax					
23. Waste Disposal					

ADMINISTRATIVE AND COMMUNICATIONS

	1958 Actual	1959 Proposed	1959 Actual	1960 Proposed	1960 Total
24. Synagogue Bulletin					
25. Supplies and Postage					
26. Office Secretary Salary					
27. Telephone					

PROPOSED INCOME – 1960

	1959 Proposed	1959 Actual	1960 Proposed
1. Membership Dues			
2. Interest on Mortgages			
3. Memorials			
4. Rentals			
5. Cemetery, Plots and Interments			
6. Sisterhood Donation			
7. Miscellaneous Donations			
8. Holiday Tickets			
9. Hebrew Instruction			
Total expenditures 1960			
Total income 1960			
Deficit			

It is the recommendation of this Committee to increase dues as follows for 1960:

35 and over
30 to 34
Under 30

Line #1 of the Proposed Income for 1960 reflects the dues expectancy with current rates with our present membership. By adopting the proposed dues increase, approximately $7,000.00 in additional dues will result based on our present membership, thereby offsetting the indicated deficit.

VII Financial Planning –
Future Security

THROUGHOUT HISTORY JEWS HAVE MADE COMMUNITY RESPONSI-
bility a part of everyday living. At the center of our community organization stands the synagogue, from which emanate spiritual
and ethical influences affecting the development of every civilization.

Our ideals, however, cannot be achieved by mere wishes or
words or pious desires. A constructive and forward-looking financial program for the contemporary synagogue is required so that
it may remain a living force, clothing its traditions in modern
garb for the enlightenment of the children, the adolescents, and
the adults.

Because we recognize that the synagogue is essential to Jewish
life, we can visualize no better way to assure the future of the
synagogue and to perpetuate the fruits of its labors than by financial planning that is concerned not only with current needs (balancing the budget), but includes as well a long-range program.

We have taken note of the wise policy of colleges, universities,
hospitals, and many historic American churches in providing sol-
id financial support for their labors of instruction, healing, ministry, and service. The generosity of the benefactors of these insti-
tions has furnished a strong bulwark against the vicissitudes of
changing economic conditions. As a consequence, their work of
truth and mercy need never be curtailed, impaired, or hampered.

The most helpful and influential institutions of our country
could not have endured, flourished, and expanded without the
generous financial provisions of contributors who have looked
ahead in their own day to the future. We are convinced that the
American synagogue merits the same foresight and statesmanship.

Rabbi Jacob J. Weinstein of K.A.M. Temple, Chicago, put it
this way:

HAVE YOU DONE JUSTLY BY THE
MOTHER INSTITUTION OF ISRAEL?

From time to time, it is my unhappy duty to listen to the
complaints of older folks who feel that they are being neg-

lected by their children. On rare occasions, the complaint
is that the children, having grown prosperous, have even
failed to share their prosperity by making the old folks a
little more comfortable. You can well understand that there
are few tasks amidst the variety that come to me in my calling that are more repugnant than this, of having to remind
sons and daughters of their obligations to their parents.

In a less personal, though no less poignant, way, the synagogue — the mother institution of Israel — makes the same
complaint. She sees her daughter institutions — the charities, the welfare funds, the defense organizations — richly,
sometimes lavishly, maintained, while she is fed on strict
economy rations. These daughter institutions take capital
reserves, unemployment insurance, sickness benefits, sever-
ance pay, retirement funds in their strides. The synagogue
still, for the most part, finds itself outside the circle of these
modern safeguards against catastrophe. I have heard of instances where certain individuals have given $25,000 to the
United Jewish Appeal and $100 to their synagogue.

Even if the synagogue were only the source and inspiration of the good works of our society, it would, on sentimental grounds alone, deserve better treatment from our people.
But the fact is that the synagogue is still the central identify-
ing agency for the Jewish people . . . .

It is a sad commentary on the financial history of our congregations that by and large our Boards of Trustees have not been in
the habit of looking very far ahead, but have usually been content
to come out even or almost even at the end of each fiscal year,
letting the future take care of itself. Yet, financial planning in the
contemporary synagogue must not only envisage the provision of
an income that will be adequate to support a program of activity
and service in a given year, but also the building of reserves to secure its future existence. This long-range phase of financial planning stands on its own and does not compete in any way with efforts being made in a congregation to obtain its operational income, as will be indicated later.

It is hardly to be expected that reserve funds will be built up in
the synagogue from dues or other regular income. A planned financial program should, therefore, look beyond the income from

the so-called regular sources for the creation and building up of these reserves.

The following are a few of these potential sources of income:

1. Bequests to the synagogue in wills of members.
2. Naming the synagogue as a beneficiary in insurance policies.
3. Creating charitable trusts for the benefit of the synagogue.
4. Establishment of endowments.
5. Contributions of stocks and bonds.
6. Contributions of real estate or other property.
7. Annual contributions from private and corporate foundations.
8. Annuities.
9. Outright substantial gifts.

Most of these sources of income require highly specialized forms of fund-raising, and you will need the advice and guidance of a committee of experts in these fields (attorneys, accountants, trust officers, insurance men). In most of our congregations this is still largely an unplowed field, and it is high time that the synagogue, large and small, claim its rightful share from these resources.

What Some of Our Congregations Are Doing

While long-range financial planning is still an "unknown quantity" in the vast majority of our congregations, it is heartening to note that a beginning in this direction has been made in a few congregations, and that there is an awakening to the necessity of building "future security" in others.

Congregation Rodeph Sholom of New York established a Foundation Fund in 1952, and in a decade acquired more than $500,000 in the Fund. Its Foundation Fund was established for the following purposes:

1. To maintain and develop our religious, cultural, educational, welfare, and communal activities in further fulfilment of the principles and ideals of our congregation;

2. To provide for major improvements in our present temple and temple house facilities, or to meet structural needs now and in the future;

3. To augment our pension and retirement resources for the members of our temple staff, including our rabbis, our professional, clerical, and maintenance workers, in accordance with our pension and retirement plan;

4. To make possible the application of gifts for special purposes in accordance with the directions of the donors, provided that the gift contributed in each instance meets the requirements prescribed by the Board administering our Foundation Fund.

For these and allied objectives the congregation seeks to establish a large capital Foundation, to be built up as rapidly as the generosity of contributors permits.

Rodeph Sholom published an attractive and well-written brochure, under the following headings:

1. Foreword
2. Purpose of the Fund
3. The Administration of the Foundation Fund
4. How Gifts Can Be Made (giving a list of sources)
5. Form of Bequest
6. List of Officers, Trustees, and Members of the Foundation Fund Committee

Since 1953, Rodeph Sholom has issued a number of supplementary pamphlets on its Foundation Fund and has made it a practice to publicize the Fund frequently in its weekly congregational bulletin. A selection of these bulletin notices is reproduced below:

OUR FOUNDATION FUND

RABBI NEWMAN has for many years advocated the establishment of an Endowment Fund and believes that the creation of our Rodeph Sholom Foundation Fund is a statesmanlike action to assure the continued growth of our congregation and its activities. Commenting on the value of the Foundation Fund, Rabbi Newman has said: "We are following in the footsteps of universities, churches, hospitals, and other institutions of education, religion, and humanitarian service, by taking steps to furnish permanent resources for our beloved Rodeph Sholom."

REMEMBER OUR FOUNDATION

MANY PERSONS remember philanthropic and religious institutions in drawing up their will, for they wish after their own lifetime to give of their substance to the perpetuation of ideals. No institution is more worthy of such support than the synagogue, which has always been dedicated to the advancement of prophetic Judaism in the community. Our temple, with its program of religious inspiration, cultural enrichment, fellowship, social service activities, and intergroup relationships, renders indispensable service in these days of crisis. No more valuable bequest can be made than one to the institution which does so much good for so many people and guides and inspires thousands to better and happier living.

— *Remember our Foundation in your will.*

PRESIDENT PROCLAIMS
FOUNDATION FUND MONTH

IN CONFORMITY WITH the far-seeing policy of leading colleges, hospitals, and churches in America in providing substantial reserves for the future, the Foundation Fund of Rodeph Sholom was established in the fall of 1952. Since that time a number of gifts have been made to the Fund and we have every assurance that substantial bequests and endowments are being contemplated in the wills of many of our congregants. The month of May is being utilized to publicize and promote our Fund and to remind our families to keep in mind our long-range program for sustaining our synagogue. Gifts to the Fund can be made by means of direct lifetime endowments, bequests in wills, the assignment of insurance policies, stocks and bonds, real estate transfers, and annual donations from private and business foundations. An advisory committee is available to discuss with our congregants any of these plans. Mr. George L. Cohen is chairman of the Foundation and Mr. Irving Levy is the co-chairman. Mr. Leo A. Diamond heads a special professional committee to promote the Fund among the attorneys, accountants, and insurance men in the temple. Mr. Falk, in his appeal to our membership, reminds us that "the most influential and helpful institutions of our country could not have endured, flourished, and expanded without the generous financial provisions of contributors who have looked ahead in their own day to the future. We in Rodeph Sholom are convinced that the American synagogue merits the same foresight and statesmanship."

Therefore, we can visualize no better way to guarantee the message of our synagogue than to perpetuate the fruits of its labors through the creation of THE CONGREGATION RODEPH SHOLOM FOUNDATION FUND.

TRUSTEES PLEDGE SUPPORT TO FOUNDATION FUND

SETTING A MEMORABLE example of synagogue loyalty, the Board of Trustees at its meeting of February 13 pledged to make individual endowments and bequests to the Foundation Fund. In affirming their confidence in the value of the plan, two of the trustees mentioned sizable bequests which they have already included in their wills for this purpose. Mr. Samuel Falk, co-chairman of the Fund, who presided at this meeting, stated: "You have this evening made a historic contribution to the future security of our congregation. We have seen in the trying days of the 1930's a curtailment of our activities and a reduction in staff which seriously affected our temple progress. Such a situation must never occur again. Our Foundation Fund will not only guarantee the advancement of our temple program but will give further encouragement to our dedicated staff — by assuring future retirement and pension arrangements. Congregants, in drawing up their will, are urged to keep the Foundation Fund in mind."

PROFESSIONAL COMMITTEE FORMED TO AID FOUNDATION FUND

TO FURTHER BRING the Rodeph Sholom Foundation Fund to the attention of our congregants and friends, a professional committee has been formed, with Mr. Leo A. Diamond as chairman, to reach the attorneys, accountants, and insurance men in our congregation. The purpose of this subcommittee is to encourage our members in these professions to reach their clients to make annual gifts, endowments, and bequests to the Fund. Serving with Mr. Diamond is a committee composed of Mr. Joseph Quittner, Murray Baron, Marcel Horowitz, Samuel Kolin, and Charles A. Tally. Mr. George L. Cohen is the over-all chairman of the Foundation Fund.

ENDOWING THE SPIRITUAL

LAST WEEK AN ANNOUNCEMENT was made by the Harvard Divinity School that John D. Rockefeller, Jr., has made a gift of $1,000,000 towards the increased vitalization of the school. In his letter notifying President Pusey of the gift, Mr. Rockefeller testified to his own belief "in the underlying importance of the spiritual life" and his confidence that President Pusey's own belief, expressed in his article, "A Religion for Today," would have "far-reaching influence on education in this country."

Although great sums have been left for secular education by philanthropists and foundations, too little attention has been directed to the needs of religious education in our school of higher spiritual instruction. Only if we can develop a vigorous and enlightened leadership in religion can we hope to preserve the ethical and spiritual values underlying the best in American and world life.

In Congregation Rodeph Sholom we can take to heart the message of Mr. Rockefeller's historic gift. Our Temple Foundation Fund has as its purpose the establishment of an adequate fund to maintain and perpetuate those ideals of religious worship and Jewish education which have made our synagogue a force for community and national good during its 112 years of service. An inspiring example has been set for us in Jewish religious life. Let us, according to our means, act upon it by participating in our Foundation Fund. If you make a gift in your lifetime and leave a bequest in your will, you will have carried forward the high objectives of our temple life.

FOUNDATION FUND GIFTS

MR. AND MRS. ROBERT BLANK have made a generous gift to our Temple Foundation Fund in honor of Mother's Day. Mr. Paul Hahn has also made a generous donation to the Foundation Fund. We are indeed grateful to these devoted members for their many benefactions to Congregation Rodeph Sholom throughout the years. Mr. George L. Cohen, chairman of the Foundation Fund committee, wishes again to emphasize the importance of remembering our Foundation Fund on all occasions in the life of our congregants. We have already received numerous gifts to the Fund from temple families and friends on occasions of marriage, Bar Mitzvah celebrations, and for special holidays. Memorial gifts are suggested as a fitting tribute to departed members of the family and friends. We invite you to do whatever you can to upbuild this vital Fund so that our temple program for religious enlightenment, social welfare, and the public good can be maintained and advanced.

FAMILY FOUNDATION

IN RECENT DAYS a letter has been sent to our temple families calling attention to the importance of our Foundation Fund. To those congregants who have family foundations, we respectfully urge the inclusion of our Temple Foundation Fund as a beneficiary. To those corporations and businesses which make annual gifts to various causes, we urge that Rodeph Sholom be not overlooked.

Let us do what we can now to see to it that our temple, worthy of the finest in our Jewish and in our American heritage, shall be the rightful possession of our posterity. Remember the temple in your long-range planning — include it significantly in your WILL.

Congregation Emanu-El of San Francisco established, in 1955, the Temple Emanu-El Fund, and published a beautiful brochure, containing suggestions to members concerning gifts and bequests.

Temple Sholom of Chicago established a Foundation Fund in

1956, and published a series of articles in its weekly bulletin, some of which are reproduced below:

WHY A FOUNDATION FUND?

THE ACTION OF THE congregation at the annual meeting on January 20, creating the Temple Sholom Foundation Fund, has caused quite a few of our members to ask why this action was taken. The answer to the question is simple and straight to the point.

The Foundation Fund has been created in order that the congregation may build up a reserve of resources in order to be prepared for any economic changes which may now, or in the future, affect the security and stability of this congregation.

We have not been able to set aside any funds from our regular income for the proverbial "rainy day." We know from experience that a "rainy day" is inevitable, whether it be a major repair job on this magnificent but aging edifice, or an economic recession which would reduce our income to such an extent that we would possibly even be precluded from opening this institution for regular worship.

Most churches of other denominations of real position in the community have long ago established their Foundation Funds. The interest from these funds, in many instances, supplements the regular income of the congregation and thus, in the long run, reduces the direct membership or assessment charges the members are required to pay.

Contributions to the Foundation Fund are tax deductible. Contributions may be made in many forms — stocks, bonds, other securities, real property, and last, but certainly not the least, cash donations.

SECURITY FOR THE TEMPLE

CONGREGATIONAL LEADERS throughout the United States have come to the realization of the fact that sporadic fund raising efforts in behalf of every special project are fast becoming a thing of the past.

These dedicated men, outstanding successes in their own business, are convinced that "The Foundation Fund," the means by which the Temple is constantly given financial support to insure its perpetuity and stability, is the only way to place any congregation on a firm financial foundation.

Although we hate to use the term "business," there is no business as vital and important as the synagogue, which is compelled to operate, year after year, on a "hand-to-mouth" basis. Each year we hope that we will receive sufficient income to avoid facing a sizable deficit. Each year we have a deficit.

Only when we have created a substantial financial endowment, which we have chosen to call the Temple Sholom Foundation Fund, and only when the income from such a fund becomes available to supplement the regular income of the congregation, will this congregation, or any congregation, be truly economically secure.

Each member of our temple should plan now to give what he can to support and establish "The Foundation Fund." Watch for the special brochure which the Foundation Fund Committee has prepared for early release. Discuss the subject with your tax advisor and your lawyer and then do the right thing.

In Baltimore, the Eutaw Place Temple received a gift of $500,000 from one individual. In New York, a bequest was made to a synagogue in the amount of $600,000. It can happen here too, because we know that we have within our great family men and women who have the means to make comparable gifts to this, their house of worship.

Temple Sinai of Oakland, California, has established a Memorial Trust Fund and has publicized it effectively in its congregational bulletin. We are quoting one of these notices.

MEMORIAL TRUST FUND

FIVE OUTSTANDING community leaders among the membership of the congregation have been appointed trustees of the Temple Sinai Memorial Trust Fund by President Philip Scheibner with the approval of the Board of Directors. The trustees of this new important function of the temple are: Joseph Altman, Nat Levy, Sol Scherman, Sidney Silverstein, Harold Strom.

The Memorial Trust Fund was approved by the membership at the last annual meeting. It will be recalled that the purpose of the Fund is to enable donors to make permanent gifts to Temple Sinai and to provide for a long-range secure method of insuring the financial security of the congregation.

The Fund invites the congregants and their friends to donate gifts to Temple Sinai for the Memorial Trust Fund. These gifts for religious purposes are encouraged by the federal and state tax laws which provide liberal deductions for income tax purposes. The trustees of the Memorial Trust Fund invite inquiries regarding all potential donations. From time to time the Bulletin will publish information of methods to make substantial donations that have been approved by tax authorities.

North Shore Congregation Israel of Glencoe, Illinois, established in 1959 an endowment fund and made the following announcement in its congregational bulletin:

OUR ENDOWMENT FUND

AFTER MORE THAN three years of study and discussion, the Board of Trustees recently established the NORTH SHORE CONGREGATION ISRAEL ENDOWMENT FUND. The idea for a separate and permanent fund for the congregation was originally proposed by Robert S. Adler while he was president. The primary purpose of the endowment is to build, during periods of prosperity, a substantial trust estate for the future benefit and security of the congregation. The principal of the Fund, barring unforeseen emergencies, will always remain intact and the income therefrom will be used for the future pension and emergency needs of our faithful and devoted employees, and for other necessary temple purposes.

Nearly $11,000, the accumulation of bequests, special gifts, and yahrzeit plaque contributions received during the past few years, have already been paid into the trust. It is our hope that by their wills and by living gifts our members will, during the years to come, build up the Fund to a substantial amount.

The Endowment Fund was established under the terms of a trust agreement authorized by the trustees and executed by the president and secretary of the congregation. One of the provisions of the instrument places the trust, in all of its aspects, under the control of an independent committee of five members of the congregation to be elected by the Board of Trustees. Two of the committee members must be trustees of the congregation, and three, non-trustees. The first committee has been elected and is comprised of Robert S. Adler, A. G. Ballenger, Zollie S. Frank, Milton J. Krensky, and John V. Spachner, all of whom are long-time and respected members of the congregation.

The Endowment Fund fills a long-felt need of the temple. An institution of our size and importance in the community should be endowed with resources sufficient to tide it over a period of lowered income, as well as to enable it to give assistance to its staff. The absence of such a reserve has been a matter of concern to the trustees. The establishment of the Fund was the first essential step towards the elimination of this concern for our future. I urge our members to keep in mind at all times the existence of our Endowment Fund so that when a philanthropic contribution is contemplated, the temple will not be overlooked.

Many thousands of men and women have found happiness and satisfaction in giving substantial sums to the religious instituion with which they are affiliated. I know that our members will be similarly rewarded by contributions to the Endowment Fund of North Shore Congregation Israel.

If you have any questions, or wish to make contributions to the Fund, any of the committee members, the trustees, Dr. Siskin, or Miss Wexelman at the temple office will be pleased to be of assistance and to answer any questions.

Rabbi William B. Silverman of Temple B'nai Jehudah, Kansas City, introduced a "Legacy of Loyalty" project during his ministry at Temple Emanuel in Duluth, Minnesota. The announcement was as follows:

THE LEGACY OF LOYALTY

A NEW AND CONSTRUCTIVE type of loyalty pledge was introduced at the annual congregational meeting of Temple Emanuel, Duluth, Minnesota, when the retiring president, Mr. Maurice Cohen, announced that almost all of the members of the Board of Trustees have made or revised a will and specified a bequest for the temple as a legacy of loyalty to foster and perpetuate the ideals of Liberal Judaism.

This unprecedented action came about as a result of a talk given by the spiritual leader of the temple, Rabbi William B. Silverman, at a meeting of the Board of Trustees. At that time, Rabbi Silverman called upon the Board to anticipate future emergencies and urged that measures be taken to secure adequate financial support for the temple. The Rabbi then suggested a "Legacy of Loyalty" project to be undertaken by the Board as a constructive and dramatic example to the entire congregation. The Board of Trustees would thus properly assume the initiative in manifesting an identification with and devotion to the temple.

The project was endorsed in principle, and a committee appointed to contact the 18 members of the Board of Trustees. Each Board member was free to participate in or abstain from the project. The matter was entirely personal and voluntary. After each Board member had been contacted, it was found that the members of the Board had predominantly chosen to participate in this project by consulting an attorney and by making or revising a will to bequeath a legacy to the temple.

After the dramatic announcement of this action at the annual meeting of the congregation, other members of the temple indicated that they, too, would join with the Board in this "Legacy of Loyalty" project, not only to provide greater financial security, but to indicate to their children and children's children their identification with and devotion to the temple, and the exalted ideals of the Jewish faith.

A number of excellent articles have appeared in temple bulletins which highlight the importance of educating the membership. Rabbi Ira Eisenstein, formerly of the Anshe Emet Synagogue, Chicago, and now of the Reconstructionist Foundation, writes:

IS THE ENDOWED SYNAGOGUE A DREAM?

IS IT POSSIBLE THAT the time may come when congregations will not be plagued by money troubles? Or is the endowed synagogue merely a messianic dream? Every year, the small band of men and women who have to worry about meeting the annual budget weave fantasies about a reserve fund from which deficits would be met, from which improvements would be made, on which the congregation could rely in periods of economic uncertainty.

Yet, it seems to me, even more fantastic is the absence of such funds. An institution which spends more than a quarter of a million dollars a year and has to live from hand to mouth, year in and year out, is an absurdity in these prosperous days. No individual would run his personal affairs this way, without insurance against disaster; yet individuals comprising the membership of a congregation permit it to drift, unmindful of what the future may bring.

I was aroused to these thoughts by two items which reached my desk in recent weeks. One was a communication from my alma mater, Columbia University (Committee on Wills and Special Gifts) ; the other was a report from Eutaw Place Temple in Baltimore to the effect that a gift of $500,000 had been made to the synagogue by one individual. Apparently, more and more people are providing in their wills for substantial gifts to religious and educational institutions, and for good reasons.

We are becoming increasingly conscious of the fact that (1) without moral and spiritual guidance, our material civilization can lead us to perdition; (2) it is the shame of our nation that the churches and synagogues live a precarious existence; (3) the government has provided extraordinary tax savings for those estates which include bequests to synagogues and churches.

May you all enjoy a happy and long life; but when the inevitable comes, may our wills bring relief to the hard-pressed survivors who are trying to run the synagogue on the income from the High Holy Days.

Rabbi Leo Bergman of Touro Synagogue, New Orleans, writes:

WILL YOUR WILL DISGRACE YOU?

IN THE PAST FEW years I have been especially interested in the wills that various men in our community have left. I have been interested in the wills of men whom I have known in other cities.

Many times I feel that the wills that some of our very prominent people leave are a disgrace to themselves, to their families, and to their good names. Allow me to explain what I mean.

When men have lived in a community for years and earned their livelihood, let alone their fortunes, in that community, it seems only the better part of intelligence and decency that some of that fortune which they leave be given back to the community from which they garnered it.

When I read how a prominent businessman, who lived in a certain community fifty or sixty years and made a fortune there, died without leaving one single solitary cent to any of the institutions in that community, I am ashamed for him, for his family, and for his friends.

When I read how doctors and lawyers who should know better, because they know the great needs of public institutions, die and leave fortunes to their children — the interest of which is to be used by their wives during their lifetime — and nothing more in their wills, I feel that very often this is a matter of thoughtlessness and selfishness.

In any city, large or small, there are social agencies, there are hospitals, there are libraries, and there are synagogues that are dependent upon the generosity and the thoughtfulness of people of means.

Recently a citizen of New Orleans died and left his church $375,000 and similar gifts to other institutions. In Brooklyn, New York, a member left his Reform temple $600,000 in his will. I do not know of any similar action in the Jewish community in this city.

The lawyers in the various congregations who help men prepare their wills can do a great deal toward guiding people in the right direction.

Immortality depends upon attaching yourself to immortal deeds and actions and institutions.

What provisions have you made in your will so that your

name may be honored among men in your community and in your city?

What are you planning to give back to a community that has given you so much?

What are you doing for your synagogue so that your name may live forever in the house of God?

Will the will you leave honor you and your family and your name? It takes so little to do a worthwhile deed. It simply takes a little thoughtfulness to immortalize yourself.

From the bulletin of the Park Synagogue, Cleveland, Ohio, comes the following:

CHARITY CAN BE A PROFIT IN DISGUISE

IT IS SURPRISING how many persons become charitable when they find it saves them money under inheritance and income tax laws. This assertion was made by Norman A. Sugarman, Cleveland attorney and former assistant commissioner of the Internal Revenue Service, when he addressed nearly 300 lawyers and insurance men at an institute of estate planning. "Persons in upper income brackets often save a lot of money by giving some of it away," he said.

Sugarman pointed out that many times persons owning real estate that had increased in value could save money by giving the property directly to charity rather than selling it and giving the money. By giving the property the owner can avoid paying a capital gains tax on the increased value which often can be quite considerable.

He described a complex procedure by which a man could set up a trust for his wife for life, with the money later going to his children and the remainder going to charity. "By tacking on this charitable remainder clause, a man can reduce the estate tax greatly," he said. "In this way he can see to it that his wife is taken care of and at the same time that the government gets no money from him. It is a choice of paying money to government or charity."

In many practical situations the charitable gift, by cutting estate taxes, can provide greater amounts of present cash for the family. He underscored that using charities to minimize taxes was far from being a trick on the government. He quoted a congressional committee report which held that if such tax savings were not allowed even greater amounts would be lost to charities.

The bulletin of the Flatbush Jewish Center, Brooklyn, New York, carried the following item:

BEQUEATHES $9,000,000

NO, NOT TO THE synagogue. But why not?

Of the primacy of the synagogue in Jewish life in America there can certainly be no doubt. That fact has been repeated and explained often enough — and is clear enough on only a moment's thought — to require repetition. How much more significant, therefore, is our institution, which includes within its edifice not only a synagogue but three religious schools, facilities for meetings of various national charitable organizations, a complete youth program for the social, spiritual, and recreational growth of our children, and adult social, educational, and recreational programs. And let us not forget the non-physical assets — the participation of our institution in annual fund-raising for more than 15 charitable and religious organizations, our own charitable contributions, and the intangible of creating an atmosphere of living Judaism within our community.

Does not all this warrant *continuing* support? A legacy can accomplish this. So many of us, aware of the uncertainties of the morrow, have made wills to provide for *continuing* aid. Have you remembered the synagogue as a beneficiary of that continuing assistance? If you have not, don't you agree — upon reflection now — that the synagogue needs and deserves such help?

There are two prevalent misconceptions that have hampered the creation of foundation and endowment funds in our synagogues. First, that this is an undertaking that is limited to the larger congregations, and second, that it is a program that is dependent upon having within the membership some very wealthy individuals. A thorough reading of the illustrations provided in this chapter should prove that both conclusions are erroneous.

While the size of the foundation or reserve fund that a congregation creates may be limited by the size of the membership, the necessity to provide for the future of the smaller congregation is even more obvious. A congregation with an annual operating budget of $50,000 requires only $1,000 in the fund to have created a reserve of 2 per cent. A congregation with an annual budget of $250,000 will have achieved a 2 per cent reserve if it secures contributions of merely $5,000.

While one may gainsay that the larger congregation will have more individuals capable of giving or bequeathing $5,000 or more to the synagogue, this program is not limited to men and women of great wealth. There are illustrations galore that by a process of education the average member of the congregation will recognize the need and respond to the plea.

REFERENCES

ANDREWS, EMERSON F., *Philanthropic Giving*, Russell Sage Foundation, 1948.
———— *Corporation Giving*, Russell Sage Foundation, 1952.
———— *Attitude Toward Giving*, Russell Sage Foundation, 1953.
———— *Philanthropic Foundations*, Russell Sage Foundation, 1956.
FLEXNER, ABRAHAM, *Funds and Foundations*, Harper and Bros., 1952.
GRANGER, WILLIAM J., *et al.*, *Wills, Executors and Trustees*, Ronald Press Co., 1950.
JENKINS, EDWARD C., *Philanthropy in America*, Association Press, 1950.
LASSER, J. K., *How Tax Laws Make Giving to Charity Easy*, Funk & Wagnalls.
WALTON, ANN D., and ANDREWS, EMERSON F., *The Foundation Directory*, Russell Sage Foundation, 1960.

VIII Securing Funds
for
Capital Needs

SINCE THE END OF WORLD WAR II OUR COUNTRY HAS WITNESSED unprecedented building programs by religious institutions. It is estimated that in 1960 alone the record sum of one billion dollars was expended on this type of construction. This tremendous activity is taking place in response to a combination of the following factors:

1. A renewed interest in the spiritual aspect of man's existence accompanied by an increase in formal affiliation, or membership, in religious institutions.

2. An increase in over-all population.

3. The changing patterns of urban neighborhoods and the continued growth of suburban communities.

4. The increased mobility of our population brought about by improved transportation facilities (highways) and the dispersion of commercial and industrial centers.

5. The obsolescence of present religious structures in relation to program requirements, as well as the normal ravages of time.

6. The emergence and availability of new products and materials which add to the functionality of the religious structure in relation to the contemporary program needs.

Faced with these factors, many synagogues contemplate building programs and find that they do not have the necessary reserve funds. Nor can these funds be secured from normal income sources without jeopardizing the operating budget of the congregation. The only satisfactory alternative for financing major capital expenditures is a well planned, well manned, well executed fund-raising campaign.

Launching the Campaign

There are four basic questions to be answered by the congregation before launching a campaign. The answers to these questions may seem deceptively self-evident to the leadership but it is essential that the membership be convinced of the soundness of the contemplated project. Failure to convince the vast majority of the membership in this regard is the most frequent cause of campaign failure. Therefore, at the very outset, the membership must respond affirmatively to the following questions:

1. Is there a demonstrable need to build or renovate?
2. Is the membership in favor of building at this time?
3. Is the proposed location the best suitable?
4. Is the plan for financing the project feasible?

It is the responsibility of the Board of Trustees to probe thoroughly every facet of these basic questions before presenting proposals to the congregation. To do this properly, committees should be appointed with the following duties and functions:

1. *Planning Committee* — to analyze thoroughly the present physical facilities and to determine their adequacy for the present synagogue program and size of membership. It will then consult with local community and business agencies to determine the probable growth of the community and its effect upon the future of the congregation. Its conclusions should be reported to the Board.

2. *Public Relations and Publicity Committee* — to inform the membership of the contemplated project and to determine whether they properly understand the current and future needs of the congregation.

3. *Site Selection Committee* — to study population distribution, zoning ordinances, room for future expansion, availability of transportation, adequacy of parking facilities, and proximity to other synagogues. Since site selection is a very technical matter, it is important that the committee secure the advice of a competent architect at this juncture. It is recommended that congregations avail themselves of the services of the Architects' Advisory Panel of the Union of American Hebrew Congregations with regard to every phase of the building and financing program.

4. *Fund-Raising Committee* — to arrive at preliminary estimates of the cost of the project in consultation with an architect. Another function of the committee is to analyze the ability of the

present and potential membership to finance the project, and to outline a fund-raising plan for securing the monies required. The committee should consider, at the appropriate juncture, the question of whether to engage professional fund-raising counsel or conduct the campaign with its own staff.

Presuming that the reports of these four committees convince the Board to advance the project, a special congregational meeting should be scheduled to secure membership understanding and approval. In preparation for this meeting, the membership should be supplied with a synopsis of the conclusions of the four committees by direct mail or through the pages of the synagogue bulletin.

Professional Fund-Raiser or Do It Yourself?

Raising money is a difficult job under the best of circumstances. It requires experience as well as certain intangible qualities and personal skills. Above all, it is exacting, time-consuming work. Particularly if the sum to be raised is large and the membership runs into hundreds of families, it is questionable whether it can be handled by the congregation's lay and professional leaders. Do they have the experience, the administrative skills, and the personal qualities required? If they do, are they able to devote the many hours required for this task without jeopardizing their business, professional, and family responsibilities?

It is a proven fact that more money is raised — and at much lower proportioned cost — with professional direction. In addition, professional direction, because of its almost uniform success, tends to enhance congregational morale. We, therefore, highly recommend that congregations give earnest consideration to engaging the services of professional fund-raising counsel. In this connection the UAHC's Commission on Synagogue Administration maintains a listing of professional fund-raising counsel who have successfully managed campaigns for synagogues and other communal institutions in all regions of the country.

The engagement of professional counsel does exactly what it

implies — provides guidance and direction along the following lines:

1. The professional organization consults with and advises congregational leadership on setting adequate goals, timing, methods to be employed, and assigns a member of its staff to the campaign with the approval of the Board.

2. The assigned professional helps to enlist and organize the working force of volunteers and trains them in the time-tested techniques of fund-raising.

3. He helps select campaign leaders.

4. He develops a campaign schedule and sees that it is adhered to.

5. He aids the volunteers in selecting assignments and conducts periodic meetings to assess the progress.

6. He develops literature on fund-raising, including available memorial gifts, contributions of securities, tax advantages, etc.

7. He devises a system of recording and collecting pledges so that the cash will be available as required to meet the construction program.

Methods and Procedures

The experience of professional fund-raising counsel has enabled us to establish certain norms and come to certain rule-of-thumb conclusions, such as:

1. The pledge period should never exceed five and preferably be limited to three years.

2. The amount that can be raised in the pledge period will usually be five times the annual operating budget of the congregation, providing that:

    a. Pledges will total one-half of the estimated giving ability of the membership, and

    b. Five per cent of the members will pledge 50 per cent of the goal, and

    c. Fifteen per cent of the members will pledge 80 per cent of the goal.

Shall the building project be abandoned if evaluation indicates that these norms cannot be approached? If the need for the facilities is definitely established, the program should go forward with the following modifications:

1. The construction program may be organized in several stages, with the most needed facilities first on the agenda.

2. Modification in plans can be made to eliminate those desirable but not essential aspects, and the substitution of less costly but equally suitable building materials.

3. Arrangements can be made to complete the project with the aid of long-term mortgage financing.

The choice of campaign personnel is of great consequence, particularly the campaign chairman. He should be a popular, dedicated, energetic man of proven communal leadership ability who will be able to give generously of his time and means. A dynamic past president with knowledge of the membership is a good example. In established congregations, the appointment of an elder statesman, with a record of generous giving, as honorary chairman, lends prestige to the undertaking.

The rabbi will play a vital role in all facets of the drive by setting the spiritual tone through his messages from the pulpit, his articles in the synagogue bulletin, and his frequent contacts with the membership. Experience has also shown that in many congregations the rabbi has been responsible for securing some of the larger pledges to the campaign.

The campaign chairman bears a heavy responsibility and it is suggested that he appoint a Campaign Cabinet to aid him in the setting of policy as well as in the supervision of the campaign structure. The Campaign Cabinet should consist, as a minimum, of the following subcommittees:

1. *Publicity Committee* — to prepare material for mailings and for the synagogue bulletin, local newspapers, as well as radio and TV outlets. Of particular importance to this committee is the job of keeping the membership informed on the progress of the campaign.

2. *Evaluation Committee* — to establish the giving potential of each member.

3. *Special Gifts Committee* — to solicit those prospects whose contribution will constitute the major share of the funds required and who, by their example, will tend to spark the campaign.

4. *General Solicitation Committee* — to be responsible for securing pledges from the membership following the publication of the results of the special gifts campaign. This aspect of the campaign is complex if for no other reason than the large numbers involved. Hence this committee must be adequately staffed along the following lines:

    a. One worker for every five prospects

    b. One captain for every team of ten workers

    c. One general for every five captains

Campaign generals will meet with their captains before the launching of the campaign, divide the list of prospects, and discuss their mutual problems and responsibilities. Each captain will be provided with the necessary Worker's Kits containing detailed instructions, promotional literature, pledge cards and report forms.

At the conclusion of the solicitation it is important that reports filter back to the generals as quickly as possible so that the Campaign Cabinet can assess the results and report to the Board on its success or failure. The membership, too, should be promptly informed of the result so that full credit and praise can be paid to workers and contributors. Following this, the Campaign Cabinet should continue to function for the purpose of systematically following up collections on pledges in order to avoid delays in the construction schedule. *It is easier to keep up than catch up!*

While it is essential that each of the synagogue's affiliates participate in and do their part in the campaign, it is important that their activities do not conflict with the campaign time-table, that their manpower (or womanpower) be not over-extended, and that the auxiliaries do not solicit minor sums for peripheral projects and hinder more liberal giving from those able to do so. Sisterhood, Brotherhood, Couples' Club, P.T.A., Junior League, and even the children of the religious school, should all be involved in the joyful act of giving and assuming their rightful role of responsibility in creating a new edifice.

None can deny that the funds needed for the design and construction of the contemporary synagogue building present a formidable challenge to the Board and the congregation. Thus, it is wise for every synagogue to approach the problem with caution and thorough preparation. However, once the decision is made on the basis of an over-riding need, it is essential that the project receive prompt and active attention. Hesitation and doubt on the part of the synagogue's leadership will readily be noted by the membership and reflected in their will to work and to give.

There are in reality two measures of success in every capital funds undertaking and each is of equal importance. Has the campaign secured enough cash and pledges to meet the cost of constructing and equipping the new edifice? Has congregational morale been enhanced and stimulated by participation in the building program?

REFERENCES

ADLER, FRANK J., *The Fundraising Campaign,* UAHC, 1957.

ANDERSON, MARTIN, *Guide to Church Building and Fundraising,* Augsburg Publishing House, 1959.

BLAKE, PETER F., *et al., An American Synagogue for Today and Tomorrow,* UAHC, 1954.

FEDER, MAX, *Temple Facilities and Their Uses,* NATA-UAHC Synagogue Research Survey #4, UAHC, 1958.

FELLOWS, MARGARET M., and KEONIG, STELLA A., *Tested Methods of Raising Money for Churches, Colleges and Welfare Agencies,* Harper and Bros., 1959.

LIPMAN, EUGENE J., and SCHOEN, MYRON E., *The American Synagogue — A Progress Report,* UAHC, 1958.

SAMUELS, JOSEPH, *Ten Commandments for Fundraising,* UAHC, 1960.

Securing the Future of Your Synagogue, Proceedings, 9th Biennial Convention, NATA, 1959.

THE FIVE PHASES OF A BUILDING CAMPAIGN

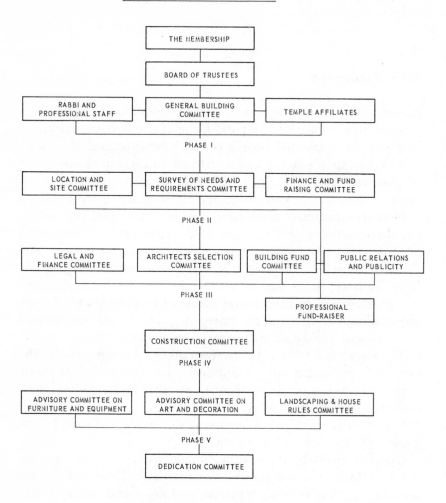

Commission on Synagogue Administration
Union of American Hebrew Congregations
838 Fifth Ave., New York 21, N. Y.

IX The Synagogue
Office

Office Management

IN THE PAST DECADE AND A HALF SYNOGOGUE AFFILIATION HAS reached new numerical heights. Congregations have striven to intensify their spiritual programs and have expanded their services. This expansion has had a marked impact upon synagogue administration. It has increased administrative tasks and has made administrative knowledge and skills all the more urgent.

Modern synagogue administration has abandoned the process of rule of thumb and the process of trial and error. It now relies on research, tested experience, guided experimentation, and the application of the scientific method to management problems. This approach has been instrumental in developing modern management principles and practices in many areas of synagogue administration and the emergence of what might be termed "the art and science of synagogue administration."

The synagogue office is the nerve center of a congregation. The office is a specialized unit of administration designed to facilitate the direct services of the synagogue. An efficiently organized, well managed, and centralized synagogue office is, therefore, one of the most important requirements in the process of sound synagogue organization and management.

Office services should have adequate, trained clerical personnel in order to make it possible for the professional staff to concentrate on their primary functions and not spend valuable time on clerical details.

The office service should be organized under central direction, with the various clerical responsibilities well defined, assigned, and supervised. The work should be carefully planned, with standards, procedures, and working methods adequately developed. Attention should be given to the personal comfort and convenience of the office staff by adequate provisions for space, lighting, heating, ventilation, noise control, rest rooms, etc. The office layout should promote the easy flow of work and allow ample spacing between desks, easy accessibility to files, and proximity of those dealing with related work. Office equipment should be modern and adequate for the purpose.

A System of Records and Forms

A major responsibility of office management is in the area of record keeping. Administration's effectiveness is dependent upon the installation of an adequate system of records and their efficient management. Records provide the objective data on the various phases of synagogue operation and are essential for planning, supervision, and decision-making. While records can be overdone, they should be adequate, reliable, and accessible. Required are standardized and simple forms, together with routine procedures for collecting the data. Provision should be made for statistically treating, summarizing, and interpreting this data periodically. Responsibility for operating the record system should be centralized.

The various types of synagogue records and forms may be classified as follows:

Corporate

    A. Articles of Incorporation

    B. Congregational Corporate Seal

    C. Constitution and By-Laws

    D. Minute Books of Meetings of Membership and Board of Trustees

Organizational

    A. Organizational Chart

    B. Staff Lists

    C. List of Board of Trustees and Boards of Auxiliary Organizations, with their terms of office

    D. Minutes of Committee Meetings

Operational

    A. Policy Book

    B. House Rules

    C. Operating Manual (by departments)

D. Personnel Practices

Personnel

A. Personal Data

B. Application

C. Work Agreement

D. Job Description

E. Salary

F. Tenure

G. Evaluation

Membership

A. Membership Application

B. Member's Permanent Family Record

C. Member's Permanent File. This is a confidential file for each individual member, filed alphabetically in a fireproof cabinet under lock. The file begins with the membership application and contains all correspondence pertaining to the member and his family.

D. Vital Statistics and Pastoral

1. Record of Births

2. Record of Consecrations

3. Record of Bar or Bas Mitzvahs

4. Record of Confirmations

5. Record of High School Graduations

6. Record of Attendance at Adult Education Classes

7. Record of Marriages

8. Record of Funerals

9. Records of Yahrzeit (alphabetical and chronological)

10. Yahrzeit Observance Reminder Notice

11. Record of Unveilings

12. Record of Visitations to the Sick

13. Record of Men in the Armed Services

14. Record of Sons or Daughters Attending Out-of-Town Colleges

15. Confidential Record of Personal Counseling (rabbi's private files)

16. Record of Conversions

E. High Holy Days

1. Unassigned Seating

    a. Card of Admission

    b. Informational Booklet About High Holy Day Regulations, etc.

    c. Record of Cards of Admission Mailed and to Whom Issued

    d. Mail Solicitations of Contributions for Yom Kippur Memorial Service Booklet

    e. Memorial Booklet

  2. Assigned Seating

    a,b,c,d,e, same as above

    f. Seating Map or Large Magnetic Grid Board

    g. Applications for Rental or Purchase of Seats

  F. Milestone and Other Remembrances

The Union of American Hebrew Congregations and the National Federation of Temple Brotherhoods have devised beautiful and inexpensive certificates and cards which can be used to good advantage to personalize important events, etc., in the life of a congregant and his family. For even greater effectiveness, the name of the congregation should be inscribed in matching type. The UAHC publishes certificates to mark the following occasions:

Circumcision	High School Graduation
Naming of a Child	Marriage
Consecration	Silver Wedding Anniversary
Bar Mitzvah	Golden Wedding Anniversary
Bas Mitzvah	Conversion
Confirmation	In Memoriam

The NFTB offers cards for the following occasions:

Birthday	New Status
Wedding Anniversary	Confirmation
Special Recognition	Speedy Recovery
Condolence	

A number of congregations, large and small, send birthday greetings each year to the member and his family as well as wedding anniversary greetings, with a personal note on the card by the rabbi. Some congregations have devised their own birthday and anniversary cards. It goes without saying that all of the above certificates and cards are not a substitute for personal pastoral ministrations but are supplementary thereto, and are usually appreciated by the congregant.

Congregations desiring to send annually birthday and anniversary cards to the member and his family should mail a questionnaire to the membership and set up simple 3x5 cards, for the record, arranged chronologically.

    G. Financial
        1. Books of Record
            a. Cash Receipt Book
            b. Check Register
            c. Accounts Receivable Ledger (Member's Dues and Contribution Record Card)
            d. Accounts Payable Ledger
            e. Purchase Book
            f. Charge Journal (Dues)
            g. Dues Adjustment Journal
            h. General Journal
            i. General Ledger
            j. Trial Balance Book
        2. Collection
            a. Statement (Wallet-type, self-mailing envelope preferred)
            b. Dues Bill Enclosures
            c. Daily Dues Collection Report
            d. Dues Collection Card (for delinquents)
        3. Office Records and Forms
            a. Receipt Book
            b. Check Book
            c. Petty Cash Envelope and Disbursement Voucher
            d. Member's Dues Adjustment Report
            e. Requisition for Purchase
            f. Purchase Order
            g. Payroll Invoice
            h. Office Invoice (departmental)
            i. Price and Source Cards or Purchase Record Card
            j. Verification and Approval Stamp for Purchase Invoice

       k. Investment Record

       l. Compensation Record

      m. Insurance Record

       n. Inventory Record (office supplies, books for sale, etc.)

    4. Tribute (Happy Day and In Memoriam) Funds

       a. Receipt (to donor)

       b. Contribution Form

       c. Acknowledgment Card (to family honored)

       d. Descriptive Booklet

    5. Auditor's Report

It is urged that the books of the congregation be audited semi-annually or annually by an independent, professional accountant (preferably by a C.P.A.). The auditor's report constitutes the official financial report of the congregation.

It is recommended that the auditor's report contain, among others, the following:

       a. Statement of Assets and Liabilities

       b. Comparative Statement of Actual Receipts and Disbursements with budgets of current fiscal year and the new fiscal year

       c. Analysis of Dues Structure

       d. Analysis of Accounts Receivable (dues) as to ages of balances

       e. Statement of Investments

       f. Schedule of Insurance on Staff Members

It is also recommended that once a year the statements to members, prepared by the bookkeeper, be *mailed by the auditor,* accompanied by a "Dues Confirmation Card" prepared by the auditor. This is an established procedure in well-conducted business concerns, is psychologically sound, and should be followed in the synagogue.

   H. Monthly Reports

    1. Bank Reconciliation

    2. Trial Balance

    3. Comparative Statement of Receipts and Disbursements (Actual and Budget Figures)

      4. Analysis of Dues Collections (Actual and Budget Figures)

      5. Statement on Tribute Funds

      6. Activity Report

I. Annual Reports

      1. Rabbi's Report

      2. President's Report

      3. Treasurer's Report

      4. Reports of Committees

      5. Reports of Affiliate Organizations

      6. Membership Report

      7. Budget Worksheet

J. Form Letters and Cards

      1. Acknowledgment of Receipt of Membership Application

      2. Acceptance into Membership

      3. Acknowledgment of Receipt of Resignation

      4. Acceptance of Resignation

      5. Collection Letters

      6. Suspension from Membership

      7. Condolence

      8. Card to Accompany Flowers Sent to a Congregant in Hospital

Office Equipment

Typewriters (preferably electric)

Duplicator

Stamping and Mailing Machine

Mailing Scale

Addressing Machine

Address Plate Maker

Letter Opener

Stapler

Paper Cutter

Multiple Paper Punch

Folding Machine

Electric Adding Machine
Check Writer
Copying Machine
Dictating Machine
Fireproof (not fire resistant) Safe
Filing Cabinets
Storage Files

Efficient Mailing Methods

Every congregation should order such publications as "29 Time-
ly Mailing Tips" issued by Pitney-Bowes, Inc. (Walnut and Pa-
cific Streets, Stamford, Conn.) and "Domestic Postage Rates and
Fees" and "Mailing Permits" from the U.S. Post Office Department (Washington 25, D.C.). These booklets will give you not
only all the information you need to know but will give you
ideas about better, more economical, and faster mail handling procedures. Every congregation should acquire a third-class
permit (1¼ cents postage) and a first-class permit (for business
reply envelopes and business reply cards). According to the present regulations of the Post Office, a piece of mail inserted in an
envelope larger than letter size (5 x 11½), or larger in either di-
mension and carrying third-class postage, *may be sealed,* thus
giving it the appearance of first-class mail. Congregations mailing weekly bulletins can obtain a second-class permit, thus getting the benefit of a low rate of postage. For details, consult your
local postmaster.

Telephone Courtesy

The business world has long recognized the importance of the
proper use of the telephone as a medium of good public relations.
Every synagogue should take advantage of the service offered
by the local telephone company and invite a representative to
meet with the secretarial staff and to show the film on the proper way of answering and making calls. The telephone company

will also be glad to make available to you the booklet, "How to Make Friends by Telephone."

Keeping Member's Family Record Up To Date

The original information for the Member's Permanent Family Record is taken from the Membership Application Blank. From that time on, the following procedure is suggested to keep this record up to date:

1. *Change of Address*

The U.S. Post Office is your best "assist" in keeping your addresses up-to-date, provided you give the Post Office Department the proper instructions.

If you wish to keep your members' addresses up-to-date, imprint on your mailing piece, "RETURN REQUESTED."

If your synagogue bulletin is mailed as second-class matter, you will automatically receive changes of address from the Post Office.

Immediately upon the receipt of an address change from the Post Office, it should be recorded on the Member's Permanent Family Record and a new address plate made.

The Post Office Department in your city will also verify all addresses and zones for you at the cost of one cent each.

Consult your Postmaster for details concerning second and third class mail.

2. *Births*

The vital statistics columns of your local newspaper and Anglo-Jewish weekly should be perused by a designated member of your staff. When a birth occurs in the family of a member, the following procedure should be followed:

    a. Record birth on Member's Permanent Family Record

    b. Notify rabbi (to call on family or send letter of congratulations, or both)

    c. Notify religious school office (to enroll the baby in the Cradle Roll)

    d. Announce birth in synagogue bulletin

    e. Send letter of congratulations in the name of the president.

3. *Consecration, Bar Mitzvah, Confirmation, Graduation*
   Post on record as these occur.

4. *Engagements*
   a. Notify rabbi (to call on family or write a letter of congratulations, or both)
   b. Announce engagement in synagogue bulletin
   c. Send letter of congratulations in name of president.

5. *Marriages*
   a. The rabbi's secretary should fill out in duplicate a "Marriage Record," original to be retained in the rabbi's office and duplicate to be turned over to the synagogue office.
   b. Synagogue office should record marriage on Member's Permanent Family Record.
   c. Announce marriage in synagogue bulletin
   d. Send letter of congratulations in name of president.

6. *Significant Anniversaries, etc.*
   a. The synagogue office should be on the alert for significant events in the lives of congregants (important wedding anniversaries, community honors, etc.) and this information should be communicated promptly to the rabbi and president.
   b. Announce these events in the synagogue bulletin.

7. *Resignation of Members*
   a. Notify rabbi, president, school office, affiliate organizations promptly.
   b. Remove address plate.
   c. Remove Member's Permanent Family Record and file same in transfer file (*do not destroy record*).
   d. Remove all other subsidiary records pertaining to resigned member.

8. *Death*
   a. Rabbi's secretary should prepare in duplicate "Funeral Record," original to be retained in rabbi's office and duplicate to go to synagogue office. If rabbi does not officiate at funeral, the synagogue office should notify the rabbi's office about the death (for condolence call by rabbi).
   b. Remove address plate. Make new plate for survivor.

    c. Make proper notation on Member's Permanent Family Record.

    d. Remove all subsidiary records pertaining to deceased.

    e. Write condolence letter in the name of the president.

    f. Announce death in synagogue bulletin.

9. *Hospitals and Funeral Director*

    a. Arrangements should be made with local hospitals to notify the synagogue office when a member of the congregation enters the hospital. A special card may be provided for this purpose.

    b. If this is not feasible, an effort should be made to obtain the list of all Jewish patients and then select from this list the names of members who are patients in the hospital.

    c. Arrangements should be made with local Jewish funeral directors to notify the synagogue office of members and relatives of members whose funerals they are handling.

The procedures suggested above are intended to facilitate the pastoral work of the rabbi and lay visitation committees.

While much emphasis must be placed upon the mechanical in considering the synagogue office, we must bear in mind the admonition of Henry Fruhauf, comptroller of Congregation Emanu-El of the City of New York. In a lecture on the synagogue office and its personnel, given as part of a course on administration for the contemporary synagogue in 1960, he said:

> Important and valuable as the contributions made by scientific developments have been and will continue to be, management of the office is primarily and basically an art and not a science. The science of business procedures is extremely important, but in the final analysis work is accomplished not by systems, rules, or procedures, but by people. The most efficient method of procedure, in my experience, is the one which will inspire people to do the best job of which they are capable . . . . To obtain the maximum results it is necessary that we establish good procedures and methods, but we will find that enthusiastic people will do better work, even with poor procedures, than will unenthusiastic workers with good procedures.

REFERENCES

FREEHOF, LOUIS J., *Manual for Double and Successive High Holyday Services*, UAHC, 1955.

GOLD, LEONARD, *The Addressograph and Temple Administration*, UAHC, 1955.

KELLOG, GRAHAM M., *Preparing the Office Manual*, American Management Association, 1959.

LITTLEFIELD, C. L., and PETERSON, R. L., *Modern Office Management*, Prentice-Hall, Inc., 1956.

MONDELL, MILTON M., *Recruiting and Selecting Office Employees*, American Management Association, 1956.

ODELL, MARGARET K., and STRONG, EARL R., *Records Management and Filing Operations*, McGraw-Hill Book Co., 1947.

PAYNE, MARJORIE T., *File This, Please!*, Dartnell Corporation, 1955.

Synagogue Reference Forms, NATA-UAHC, 1954, Revised 1963.

WEEKS, BERTHA M., *How to File and Index*, Ronald Press, 1946.

WELD, CHRISTOPHER M., *Office Manager's Handbook*, Dartnell Corporation, 1958.

X The Construction
and Maintenance
of Synagogue Buildings

OUR COUNTRY HAS BEEN WITNESS TO A PHENOMENAL CONSTRUCTION boom that encompasses every aspect of our economy and our culture. Suburban homes, city apartment houses, office skyscrapers, and factories go up on every side. Side by side with this development, a veritable wave of institutional structures: new schools, community centers, and religious buildings.

In 1945, few, if any, studies had been made of the requirements of the synagogue program. Few, if any, were the architects, engineers, and builders with a backlog of experience and knowledge in this type of structure. If the American Jewish community was to have synagogue buildings that would inspire religious feeling and reflect our religious heritage, and at the same time provide for its contemporary program needs, it would be necessary to probe the past, collect the data and facts of the present, and ponder carefully the future.

Thus it was that Rabbi Jacob D. Schwarz, then director of the Commission on Synagogue Activities of the Union of American Hebrew Congregations, called the first national conferences on synagogue architecture in Chicago and New York in 1947. To these meetings came the professionals — the architects, engineers, and builders, as well as lay and rabbinic leaders whose congregations were contemplating or in the throes of building. Avidly they digested the known facts and propounded questions and sought to find the solutions.

These initial architectural conferences proved to be of historic importance, for they produced results of a permanent and enduring nature. They highlighted the need for more direct technical assistance and for the creation of a body of literature and guides, so that the vast expenditure of resources would produce synagogue structures that would meet contemporary needs and incorporate the most inspiring and esthetic aspects of our faith.

The UAHC today continues to meet this need in the following ways:

1. *Technical Assistance*

At the outset this was provided by the devoted service of an outstanding American architect, Harry M. Prince, F.A.I.A. Alone and at great personal sacrifice, he volunteered his services as a consultant to those congregations who sought advice and aid. When it became physically impossible for one man to bear the burden, it was his example and inspiration that made possible the creation of the UAHC's Architects' Advisory Panel. Today this panel has a roster of distinguished architects from all parts of our land who have had experience in the creation of the contemporary synagogue building. It renders a unique consultation service to scores of congregations each year, and the beautiful and functional synagogues which dot our cities and suburbs reflect the importance of its mission.

2. *Publications*

The creation of a synagogue building is more involved than raising the funds and gathering the bricks and supplies. Where do we start? What do we want in our synagogues? These are the questions that troubled the Building Committees. Thus was launched another unique project — the publication of a volume that would provide the insights into the history and evolution of the synagogue structure and at the same time bring to the attention of those currently involved in creating the contemporary synagogue the best in present-day design, materials, and functional techniques. The result was the publication by the UAHC of *An American Synagogue for Today and Tomorrow,* edited by Peter Blake. Beginning with a history of synagogue architecture and art, it contains chapters on every aspect and facet of synagogue design, replete with photographs, floor plans, and ideas to guide the layman and professional alike in their efforts to glorify and serve our faith in the twentieth century.

Ten years later, in 1957, the time had come, it was felt, to assess the results of its efforts in this area, and to make a progress report. Thus it was that the second National Conference on Synagogue Architecture and Art was held in New York City. Reflecting its development in depth, the Architects' Advisory Panel included an extensive exhibit of synagogue architecture and art of the preceding decade. The deliberations of this gathering of architects, artists, lay and rabbinic leaders proved to be a valuable and informative exchange of ideas. Under the title, *The American Synagogue — A Progress Report,* the proceedings of this three-day conference have been published by the UAHC and will prove helpful to congregations launching building programs.

Equipment Reserves

With such vast amounts of money, energy, and time being mobilized for the creation of synagogue buildings, it is discouraging to find that congregations fail frequently to provide adequately in their fund-raising for the increased cost of running their buildings and in their annual operating budgets for the proper care and maintenance of the structure. There should be an annual budgetary allocation to provide for the personnel and materials to maintain maximum standards of appearance, cleanliness, safety, and repair of the building.

Business and professional people are well aware that the furniture, fixtures, machines, and tools they utilize in earning their livelihood are subject to deterioration and it is accepted practice to provide for this eventuality. Thus, they set aside each year in a reserve fund a sum which, if measured over the expected life span of the item, will provide for its replacement. Step two, therefore, should be an annual budgetary allocation to an *Equipment Reserve Fund* for the specific purpose of replacement.

Building Depreciation

Regardless of the age of the synagogue building, every congregation should set up a depreciation schedule for its major components. The passing of time will inevitably bring about a situation where repairs will no longer meet the situation. Step three, therefore, should be the creation of a depreciation schedule and the allocation in the budget of an adequate percentage of this annual depreciation charge for replacement and repairs. The age of the building will determine the depreciation factor and must of course be in proportion to the cost of the component factors and the degree of its current use.

Insurance Coverage

Public buildings and institutional structures are subject to many hazards both from man and the elements. Also, they are subject to much abuse, whether intentional or accidental, and despite the most stringent inspections and supervision, accidents will happen. The synagogue must protect itself and also, in good conscience, protect the public. It must also provide itself with assurance that despite any emergency it can continue to function and serve its members. Such assurance can only come from adequate insurance. Therefore, it is essential that every congregation prepare and maintain an insurance check list. To accomplish this end a committee should be empowered to call in a professional building appraiser to inspect the premises from basement to roof. This will provide the Board of Trustees with professional guidance as to amount of insurance required.

What are the chief risks to be concerned with in the synagogue structure? While the list could be extended, the following are the major areas of concern suggested by Sidney Margolis, executive director of Beth El Temple, New Rochelle, New York:

1. Fire Insurance — Building and Contents
   a. Extended Coverage Endorsement (Actual Cash Value)
   b. Rabbi's Home Coverage
   c. Additional Extended Coverage Endorsement (Actual Cash Value) — $50 Deductible — On Rabbi's Home Only
   d. Vandalism and Malicious Mischief Endorsement
   e. Water and Smoke Damage
2. Rental Insurance
   a. Use and Occupancy Loss
   b. Extra Expense
3. Public Liability Insurance, General and Complete
   a. Comprehensive Liability and Property Damage

   b. Owners-Landlords and Tenants Coverage (Limited)

   c. Product Liability Coverage (Limited)

   d. Elevator Liability Coverage (Limited)

   e. Owners Protective Liability Coverage (Limited)

   f. Builder's Risk

   g. Medical Payments Endorsement (Not in New York State)

4. Automobile Liability Coverage (Non-Ownership Auto Liability and Property Damage) — Subject to Audit

   a. Medical Payments

   b. Comprehensive Coverage

5. Boiler and Machinery Coverage

   a. Steam and Pressure Tanks

   b. Refrigerators, Air Conditioning, and Miscellaneous Electrical Apparatus

6. Church Burglary, Robbery, Theft and Larceny (Specification Schedule) — Charity Funds Not Covered

   a. Checkroom Coverage (See Bailee's Law)

   b. Innkeeper's Insurance (Restricted)

7. Fine Arts Policy (Scheduled Items Should Be Excluded from Fire Contents Policy)

   a. Ritual Articles

   b. Libraries

   c. Works of Art

   d. Organ and Allied Machinery

8. Glass Policy (Actual Cash Value)

   a. Plate and Stained Glass (Schedule)

9. Valuable Records Coverage

10. Blanket Fidelity Bond (Set Limits)

   a. Employees and Officers, Committee Chairmen

   b. Employees Only

11. Workmen's Compensation (Subject to Annual Audit)

12. Accident and Health Insurance

   a. Hospitalization

   b. Loss of Income

   c. Medical and Surgical

13. Miscellaneous Coverages

   a. Customer's Goods

   b. Rain Insurance — Bazaars, Carnivals

   c. Safe Burglary Insurance
   d. Camp Medical and Polio Coverage (Audit) — Summer and/or Day Camp
   e. Epidemic Refund Camp Insurance 2 per cent (Audit) — Summer and/or Day Camp

Proper insurance coverage is not a one-time or some-time program, particularly in this era of rising costs. Proper insurance coverage means to provide for replacement at present day costs, less depreciation. Thus, it is evident that the insurance program of a synagogue must be re-surveyed at regular intervals and such changes made as prove necessary and prudent.

Maintenance of Building

The synagogue building is a community institution and its facilities are utilized day and night and, in many instances, seven days a week, by hundreds of people, both young and old. Thus it is subject to much abuse as well as use. It is, therefore, of paramount importance that much thought be given to its proper maintenance. In this era of advancing costs of labor and materials, it becomes essential that we approach the problem scientifically, selecting our custodial staff with care and purchasing those labor-saving machines and devices which will reduce costs and increase efficiency.

The responsibility for implementing this program of maintenance is properly lodged in the synagogue's House Committee. The chairman of this vital committee should be chosen with care. The membership roster of the congregation should be explored for a person with a background in real estate management, engineering, architecture, construction, institutional administration, or related fields. The personnel of this committee should be chosen for their experience and interest in these fields or other aspects of the synagogue's structure.

The House Committee has the following major functions:
1. Selection of building superintendent and custodial staff
2. Promulgating House Rules and Regulations

3. Creating custodial work schedules
4. Purchasing materials and equipment
5. Supervision of a maintenance program
6. Annual review of insurance coverage

Selection of Personnel

a. Superintendent or Chief Custodian — Every congregation should have a man with experience in the operation and maintenance of an institutional structure. Upon the choice of this person may rest the success or failure of the proper maintenance of the building. Experience has shown that, to a great degree, securing a competent man will be dependent upon payment of an adequate salary and providing adequate living quarters on the premises. Since the typical synagogue program knows few holidays or hours, providing living quarters on the premises is assurance that the building will be properly supervised and protected at all times.

b. Maintenance Staff — An adequate staff must be provided to cover day, night, and week-end activities. The intensity of the synagogue program, as well as the size of the congregation, will determine the number. However, the efficiency and quality of the personnel will usually be directly related to the salary, hours, and facilities provided these important synagogue personnel. It is essential for proper maintenance that this group receive prevailing wages and hours of work, as well as be provided with an area for the storage of clothing and personal effects. Note must be made that the custodial staff is in frequent contact with the membership, both youth and adult, and, therefore, great care should be taken in their selection.

House Rules and Regulations

Definitive rules and regulations covering the use of the synagogue's facilities by the members, the auxiliaries, and outside organizations should be drawn up in consultation with the synagogue professional executive and/or the building superintendent or custodian. This will eliminate abuse and overuse of the facilities and go far towards reducing repair and maintenance costs. (Samples of House Rules can be found in the UAHC-NATA Synagogue Research Survey #4 on *Temple Facilities and Their Uses.*)

Publication and distribution of these rules on frequent occasions will educate all concerned and will guide the staff. These rules should be evaluated at frequent intervals so as to insure their adequacy.

Work Schedules and Inspections

To assure proper maintenance and repair of the building, the superintendent or custodian should be required to create a rigid and definite work schedule for the custodial staff. This schedule should be based upon close observation of the various facilities of the synagogue so that each and every facet is covered at regular intervals and at such days and hours to assure the readiness of the facility in accordance with the synagogue calendar.

Sidney S. Margolis, executive director of Beth El Congregation, New Rochelle, New York, suggests the following aids to the Building Committee:

> With the tremendous increase in synagogue building, the need for expert guidance and knowledge of new building materials has increased in the same proportions. Congregations all over the land require the services of qualified personnel in handling their newly built properties. Roughly, for our purposes, it would be advisable to break the building maintenance work into the following categories:
> 1. Scheduling and Inventory
> 2. Housekeeping
> 3. Inspection and Repair
> 4. Mechanical Services
>
> These four categories take no particular order, as they constitute an overlapping and continuing program . . . . Whether the building be a one-man or twelve-man operation, a work and time schedule is essential. This means a posting by the custodian with the director or secretary of a work hours schedule for himself and staff . . . .
>
> Your day-to-day housekeeping is without a doubt the most important single section of the entire program. This is the time, that if well and capably spent, will save you the countless hours of repair work and dollars. Good housekeeping and preventive maintenance can anticipate deterioration and prevent costly breakdown of equipment and furnishings.
>
> It is advisable that you regularly inspect the building with

the custodian and chart the necessary repairs and designate the order of priority. This regular inspection will be a deterrent to slovenliness on the part of your maintenance staff and serve to catch minor shortcomings before they become major repairs.... Your top man must certainly be qualified by experience and training to correct all minor electrical, plumbing, heating, and carpentry faults himself.... He should be able to supervise and carry through, as well as know the latest and best in building management. So choose carefully and considerately when engaging your custodian.

You can best show your pride in your synagogue building by keeping it clean and ready to use. Study how to improve and program this work on a long-term basis. This will save you heartache and embarrassment occasioned by breakdown and costly repair.

The job of maintaining our synagogue buildings so that they serve their manifold uses and still remain structures of dignity and beauty is a complex one. In the smaller synagogue, with a limited custodial staff, the responsibility falls heavily on the Building or House Committee chairman. In the larger congregation, the responsibility falls into the hands of the chief custodian. Whoever has this responsibility should be sure that he is taking advantage of the latest information and guidance available in the field of building management and maintenance.

Purchase of Materials and Equipment

While it is impossible to cite all of the do's and don't's, the experience of those entrusted with the maintenance of institutional buildings provides the following guide:

a. The use of *water* as a cleansing agent should be reduced to a minimum as it will bring about deterioration of such materials as wood, tiles, terrazzo, cement, cork, compositions, and linoleums, all of which are commonly found in buildings.

b. *Wax* is the best preservative, lessens washing and scrubbing, reduces labor, and improves with time. Liquid wax, which contains a cleaning agent as well, is the most practical and easiest to apply. Hard paste wax should be used for the first coat of flooring.

c. A good *disinfectant* should be used daily in all washrooms. Deodorants have no value but to disguise odors that cannot be removed by ventilation.

d. *Tissues* and *towels* are a major item. Competition is keen in this field. Check and experiment with sources for dispensers and do not buy until you have found the dispenser suitable for your use. Arrange to purchase your supplies of paper goods in large bulk lots so as to take advantage of quantity discounts.

e. Cleansing agents for *glass* and *windows* should be chosen with care. Avoid solutions containing alcohol as they will dissolve paint and putty.

f. *Brooms* and *mops* are ineffective as well as unhealthy. The purchase of adequate *vacuum cleaners* and floor *scrubbing machines* should be made on the basis of the type and extent of the carpeting and flooring of the building. Rugs should be cleaned by a commercial rug cleaner at regular intervals, depending upon use, and wherever possible put in rug storage for the summer months. Carpeting should be treated each year with moth destroying spray.

g. *Lighting fixtures* and *bulbs* constitute a considerable expenditure in the maintenance budget of some synagogues. Experiments with long-life incandescent and fluorescent tubes should be conducted and a record kept to determine the best brand. The cheapest can often prove to be the most expensive in the long run. By keeping accurate records of the type, size, and average life of bulb or tube, it will be possible to order the synagogue's requirements in bulk and secure quantity discounts.

h. *Kitchen equipment* must be kept immaculately clean to assure adherence to local sanitary and health codes. Experiments with cleansers and detergents for manual or machine washing of dishes, glassware, and cutlery will lead to the choice of brand and enable the placing of bulk orders at discount prices.

Proper receptacles for disposal of garbage and waste should be available so as to eliminate insect and animal life problems. A service contract with a professional *exterminator* will assure the control of this frequent problem.

i. *Organs* and *pianos* should not be serviced by the custodial staff but by experts. A maintenance contract will prove economical and will insure the proper functioning of these important adjuncts of the synagogue facility.

j. *Landscaping* and *grounds* are the face of the synagogue that everyone sees, and should always be most attractive. The equipment necessary to accomplish this purpose will vary from congregation to congregation but unless you have a superintendent with the proverbial "green thumb," it is wise to have a seasonal contract with a professional firm of gardeners to provide pruning, fertilizing, and spraying.

k. *Painting* of certain areas of the synagogue will be required on an annual basis. Keep in mind that labor costs are four times the cost of paint. It is false economy to use cheap paint since it will shorten the periods between painting.

l. *Heating* and *ventilation* of the synagogue are a major expense and, therefore, should receive much attention from the custodial staff and the House Committee. All members of the custodial staff should receive a briefing and demonstration on the proper operation and maintenance procedure by an authorized representative of the manufacturer of the equipment. Thus, each individual will be familiar enough with the system to take charge should an emergency arise.

Every car owner has his vehicle serviced and checked at periodic intervals by a competent service man to assure its efficient and safe operation. The heating and ventilation of your synagogue is in use almost every day and every hour of the year. It, too, requires frequent service and inspection of its highly complex components. It is recommended that you have a maintenance contract with a qualified heating and ventilation concern providing for periodic inspection, servicing, and repairs as needed. Failure to maintain this aspect of the building equipment may involve the synagogue in waste of fuel, deterioration of costly equipment, and failure to provide the comfort which your members expect when in the synagogue building.

m. *Plumbing* emergencies can be costly and annoying. The custodial staff should be familiar with the location of all shut-off and supply valves. Except for minor repairs, it is advisable to secure the aid of the best plumbing specialist available.

The House Committee should familiarize itself with local *fire department rules and regulations* and there should be no compromise with compliance. Fire drills should be held regularly in the religious school. Exit signs, fire alarms, fire extinguishers, and other fire prevention and fire fighting equipment should be checked frequently and placed in a conspicuous place. Fire escapes and fire exists should always be in good repair and free of impediments. The capacity limits of all rooms in the synagogue should be posted and the number never exceeded.

"Safety First" should be more than a motto in the synagogue building. Stairs and floor surfaces should be slip-proof. Adequate illumination of stairs and corridors should be provided. Snow and ice removal of walks and paths about the synagogue should be attended to immediately.

In summary, there are five basic requirements for a good maintenance program:

1. A synagogue Board that understands and appreciates the complexity of the situation.

2. A House Committee with good leadership and the will to work.

3. An adequate budgetary allowance.

4. An adequate and efficient custodial staff.

5. A conscientious application of the best maintenance techniques and materials available.

REFERENCES

BLAKE, PETER F., et al., An American Synagogue for Today and Tomorrow, UAHC, 1954.

BRAUN, ISADORE H., Jewish School Building Manual, Board of Jewish Education, Chicago, 1954.

FEDER, MAX, Temple Facilities and Their Uses, NATA-UAHC Synagogue Research Survey #4, UAHC, 1958.

GOLDSTEIN, HENRY, Coordinating the Maintenance Schedule with the Temple Program, Proceedings, NATA 8th Workshop Conference, UAHC, 1956.

HERZOG, MYRON E., Insurance Programming for the Temple, UAHC, 1952.

MURRAY, JOSEPH C., Maintenance Contracts — When and Why? Proceedings, NATA 8th Workshop Conference, UAHC, 1956.

SCHWARZ, JACOB D., Synagogue Inventory and Appraisal, UAHC, 1952.

SMALLEY, D. E., Floor Maintenance Manual, Trade Press Publishing Co., 1957.

MAINTENANCE SCHEDULE OF SPECIAL AREAS

	FLOOR		WOODWORK		FURNITURE	
	Mopped	Waxed	Dusted	Polished	Dusted	Polished
Sanctuary						
Pulpit furniture						
Choir loft						
Lobby						
Checkroom						
Social hall						
Social hall stage and rear area						
Lounge						
Kitchen						
Library						
Corridor						
Corridor						
Corridor						
Stairway						
Stairway						
Offices						
Toilet						
Toilet						
Toilet						
Classroom						
Classroom						
Classroom						

Instructions: Indicate in appropriate space date when work was done.

Example: If work was done on December 1, 1961, write 12/1/61.

OFFICE OF SYNAGOGUE ADMINISTRATION
Union of American Hebrew Congregations
838 Fifth Avenue   New York 21, N.Y.

SYNAGOGUE INSURANCE GUIDE AND CHECK LIST

Type of Insurance	Date of Policy	Term and Rate	Insurance Company	Limits	Years in Force	Last Review
1. Fire Insurance — Building and contents A. Extended Coverage Endorsement (ACV) B. Rabbi's Home Coverage C. Additional Extended Coverage Endorsement (ACV) $50.00 deductible Rabbi's Home only D. Vandalism and Malicious Mischief Endorsement E. Water and Smoke Damage						
2. Rental Insurance A. U and O Loss B. Extra Expense						
3. Public Liability Insurance General and Complete A. Comprehensive Liability and Property Damage B. O-L and tenants Coverage (Limited) C. Product Liability Coverage (Limited) D. Elevator Liability Coverage (Limited) E. Owners Protective Liability Coverage (Limited) F. Builder's Risk G. Medical Payments Endorsement (Not in New York State)						
4. Automobile Liability Coverage (Non-Ownership Auto Liability and Property Damage) Subject to Audit A. Medical Payments B. Comprehensive Coverage						
5. Boiler and Machinery Coverage A. Steam and Pressure Tanks B. Refrigerators, Air Conditioning and Miscellaneous Electrical Apparatus						
6. Church Burglary, Robbery, Theft and Larceny (Specification Schedule) (Charity Funds not covered)						

(Continued next page)

SYNAGOGUE INSURANCE GUIDE AND CHECK LIST (Continued)

Type of Insurance	Date of Policy	Term and Rate	Insurance Company	Limits	Years in Force	Last Review

6. (Continued)
  A. Checkroom Coverage (See
    Bailee's Law)
  B. Innkeeper's Insurance
    (Restricted)						

7. Fine Arts Policy (Scheduled)
  Exclude from Fire Contents Policy
  A. Ritual Articles
  B. Libraries
  C. Works of Art
  D. Organ and Allied Machinery						

8. Glass Policy (ACV)
  A. Plate and Stained Glass
    (Schedule)						

9. Valuable Records Coverage						

10. Blanket Fidelity Bond (set limits)
  A. Employees and Officers,
    Committee Chairmen
  B. Employees only						

11. Workman's Compensation (Subject to Annual Audit)						

12. Accident and Health Insurance
  A. Hospitalization
  B. Loss of Income
  C. Medical and Surgical						

13. Miscellaneous Coverages
  A. Customer's Goods
  B. Rain Insurance — Bazaars,
    Carnivals
  C. Safe Burglary Insurance
  D. Camp Medical and Polio
    Coverage (Audit)
    Summer and Day Camp
  E. Epidemic Refund Camp
    Insurance 2 per cent (Audit)
    Summer and/or Day Camp						

RULES AND REGULATIONS GOVERNING
THE USE OF THE BUILDING AND FACILITIES
OF
TEMPLE EMANU-EL, THE REFORM TEMPLE OF THE NORTH SHORE
393 ATLANTIC AVENUE

A.   Unless hereinafter otherwise provided or unless, in any particular instance, the requirements of such procedure shall have been waived by the House Committee, the congregation's synagogue and religious school building and/or the facilities thereof shall not be used in whole or in part by any person or organization other than by or for the congregation itself or by or for an auxiliary association or activity unit of the congregation except in accordance with the application procedure as hereinafter set forth.

1.   Every application shall be made upon such form only as shall have been approved by the House Committee and shall be submitted to the House Committee thirty (30) days at least before the date of intended use.

2.   Any applicant desiring to engage the services of any employee or employees of this congregation in connection with the use of the area and/or facilities desired shall

- 1 -

so specify in the application, and, if the application is allowed, the services of such employee or employees shall be at the expense of the applicant.

3. No application shall be considered by the House Committee unless there be submitted therewith a cash deposit of not less than fifty (50%) per cent of the minimum contribution established by the Board of Trustees as appropriate or requisite to cover maintenance and service costs and expense of the facilities required by the applicant.

4. No application shall be approved by the House Committee unless the names and addresses of all and any caterers, decorators, entertainers and/or other outside contractors intended to be engaged by the applicant be submitted with the application or within ten (10) days thereafter and unless they be duly approved by the House Committee.

5. No application shall be approved by the House Committee unless not more than fourteen (14) days after submission of such application there be received by such Committee certificates of the proposed caterer's and of each other proposed contractor's workmen's compensation, food and/or public liability insurance coverage for the date or dates of intended use.

6. Fourteen (14) days at least before the date of intended use, the applicant shall submit payment in full of the balance due of the pledged contribution as specified in the application.

7. No refund or abatement in whole or in part of a pledged contribution as specified in the application shall be made unless the House Committee rejects the application.

B.   All persons, organizations, committees or other groups, including auxiliary associations and activity units of this congregation, to whom the House Committee has granted the use of any of the facilities of the Temple's building or appurtenances shall use only the area, room or rooms and/or facilities assigned to their use, in each instance, and shall comply with all rules and regulations as herein set forth insofar as the same may be applicable.

1. Clergymen other than those directly associated with this congregation shall be permitted to officiate at religious ceremonies in the synagogue building only upon the express invitation of the Rabbi of this congregation.

2. Business meetings, rehearsals or functions other than those of an appropriate spiritual nature shall not be held in the building on the Sabbath, on Holy Days or on days of religious Festivals.

3. All activities in the building shall conclude by 12:00 o'clock midnight and the premises shall be vacated not later than 12:15 o'clock A. M.

4. Proper decorum and a reasonable standard of behavior shall be maintained and enforced by all persons and organizations using the Temple's premises while in or near the building or its adjacent areas.

- 2 -

5. Gambling for money at any time anywhere in or on the Temple's premises is strictly prohibited.

6. All by-laws and safety regulations as established by the Town of Marblehead shall be strictly observed at all times.

7. Alterations, additions or rearrangements of furnishings, draperies or decorations shall not be made without express approval of the House Committee.

8. Tacks, nails, screws, tapes, adhesives or any other means of fastening shall not be driven into or in any way placed in contact with the walls, ceilings, floors or other structural areas of the building.

9. All and any plans or schemes for temporary lighting, stage equipment and/or decorating (floral and/or otherwise) shall be submitted to the House Committee for approval ten (10) days at least before the date of intended use and, if duly approved, the same shall be installed under the supervision of the building superintendent in accordance with all applicable safety and fire laws, rules and regulations, and shall be subject to inspection and approval of the House Committee.

10. The organ shall be used only for religious services or ceremonies, for the religious school, or for rehearsals therefor provided that permission for such use shall have been first obtained from the Rabbi or the House Committee.

11. The organ shall be used only by the official Temple organist or by one duly approved by the House Committee and by the Rabbi.

12. Whenever an outside caterer is to be engaged by an applicant, such caterer shall, fourteen (14) days at least before the date of intended use, deposit with the House Committee a certified check in the sum of fifty ($50.00) dollars (unless in any instance the Committee shall require a larger sum or waive such requirement), the same to be held as a bond to insure strict compliance by the caterer with all rules and regulations affecting the use of the kitchen facilities, equipment, dishes, utensils and appurtenances, which said deposit shall be returned to the caterer as soon as practicable following the day of use after first deducting any expense occasioned to the Temple, by reason of the caterer's failure to comply with any of these rules and regulations, for restoration of such kitchen facilities, equipment, dishes, utensils and appurtenances to the condition thereof prior to the caterer's use.

13. All persons or organizations and their caterers, as the case may be, having the use of the whole or any portion of the building or grounds or of the kitchen and/or its facilities shall leave the same, including all kitchen equipment, utensils and other physical property, in a clean and undamaged condition and see to the removal of all garbage from the premises immediately following conclusion of the affair and before the caterer leaves the premises, and shall indemnify the congregation for all loss, cost and damage resulting from failure so to do.

14. Except when the use of the kitchen facilities is by or on behalf of this congregation, maintenance personnel regularly employed by the congregation shall not be required or permitted to wash dishes.

- 3 -

15. All deliveries to and/or removals from the kitchen shall be made only by way of the "service entrance".

16. The serving of pork products and shellfish is and shall be discouraged.

17. Sale of alcoholic beverages shall be in strict compliance with law.

18. Alcoholic beverages shall not be served anywhere in or on the Temple's premises prior to any religious ceremony.

19. The giving of gratuities to personnel regularly employed by the congregation is and shall be discouraged.

20. Permission for use of linens, silver service, candelabras or other properties under the jurisdiction and control of the Temple's Sisterhood shall be obtained from the Sisterhood.

21. Employees of the congregation shall take orders only from the Rabbi (or his secretary), the president of the congregation or the chairman of the House Committee or a person duly authorized and designated by the chairman of the House Committee.

22. The congregation assumes no responsibility or liability for damage or loss of personal property of others while on the congregation's premises and all such personal property, including motor vehicles, brought or left on the premises shall at all times be at the owner's risk.

23. Tipping of checkroom and parking attendants is prohibited.

24. The House Committee shall have the right in any instance and at the expense of the applicant to require the presence on the premises of one or more police officers and/or to require the services of one or more parking attendants.

25. The chairman of the House Committee or member of such Committee delegated by him in any instance as agent shall have and hereby is vested with full authority to exercise all or any of the prerogatives and authority of the House Committee.

26. Nothing herein shall be so construed as to bar the right of appeal to the Board of Trustees of this congregation by any person or organization claiming to be aggrieved by any action or decision of the House Committee, its chairman or agent.

Per Order of the HOUSE COMMITTEE

Herbert G. Schiff, Jr.,   Chairman

Approved by the BOARD OF TRUSTEES
October 21, 1959

Robert J. Hecht,   President

- 4 -

TEMPLE EMANU-EL, THE REFORM TEMPLE OF THE NORTH SHORE
393 Atlantic Avenue, Marblehead, Massachusetts   NEptune 1-9300

APPLICATION FOR USE OF BUILDING, ETC.

Date(s) Wanted _____ Hours _____ A.M. / P.M. To _____ A.M. / P.M.

Name _____ Phone(s) _____

Address _____

Purpose _____

Facilities Required _____

No. of Persons Expected to Attend _____

Congregational Employees Required _____

The above-named Applicant hereby applies for permission to use the Temple's building and facilities as above specified and agrees that the "Rules and Regulations Governing the Use of the Building and Facilities of Temple Emanu-El, the Reform Temple of the North Shore" as printed on the reverse side of this Application, as well as all and any other restrictions or regulations endorsed hereon and initialed by the Applicant, are an integral part of the terms and conditions of this Application and will be strictly observed and complied with at all times by the Applicant.

If this Application is approved, the Applicant agrees to make a contribution of not less than $ _____ to Temple Emanu-El's general maintenance fund and submits herewith a sum of $ _____ , equal to fifty (50%) per cent of such minimum contribution, and, in addition thereto, agrees to reimburse Temple Emanu-El for the expenses of hire of police officers, checkroom and parking attendants and congregational employees, and promises to pay to the Temple the balance of such contribution together with all such other reimbursement charges on or before _____ 19 _____. (See Rules A.2; A.3; A.6).

And the Applicant further agrees to indemnify and save Temple Emanu-El harmless from any and all damage to its building, facilities and equipment, and from any and all claim for loss, injury or damage to any person or property while anywhere on the Temple's premises, including counsel fees and expenses in connection therewith in any instance.

Signed and Sealed this _____ day of _____ 19 _____.

APPROVED: (date) _____ SIGNATURE _____

Temple Emanu-El, The
Reform Temple of the North Shore   _____
By: Member ( );   Non-Member ( )

_____
Chairman/Agent of HOUSE COMMITTEE

Rule A.4 = Requires that information as to caterer, decorators, entertainers and other subcontractors be submitted to House Committee within 10 days after filing Application.

Rule A.5 = Requires that workmen's compensation, food liability and public liability insurance certificates be filed with House Committee within 14 days after filing Application.

Rule B.12 = Requires Caterer to furnish $50.00 certified check to House Committee 14 days at least before reservation date.

PLEASE NOTE: In order to retain the good will and respect of its neighbors, Temple Emanu-El respectfully requests the Applicant's full co-operation in maintaining and enforcing proper decorum when on or near the Temple's premises. (See Rule B.4)

MEMORANDUM FOR USE OF FACILITIES

NAME _____ TIME _____

EVENT _____ DATE _____

AGENT NAME _____ PHONE _____

FACILITIES _____

Number of persons expected _____ Check Room

Parking Attendant

Accepted by _____ Date _____

Copy: Temple Office
        Rabbi
        House Committee
        Agent
        Chairman

TEMPLE EMANU-EL DEPOSIT RECEIPT

Date_____

Received _____ $ _____

in cash or certified check from _____

_____ as a bond to insure strict compliance

with all rules and regulations affecting the use of the kitchen facil-

ities, equipment, dishes, utensils, and appertanences, the deposit to

be returned as soon as practicable following the day of use after first

deducting any expense occasioned to the temple by reason of failure

to comply with any rules and regulations, for restoration of such

kitchen facilities, equipment, dishes, utensils, and appertanences to

the condition thereof prior to this usage on (date)_____

in conjunction with (event) _____

Signed _____

TO: **TEMPLE EMANU-EL, THE REFORM TEMPLE OF THE NORTH SHORE**
393 Atlantic Avenue, Marblehead, Massachusetts

From: _____
            Applicant's Name and Address   Reservation Date

As required by Rule A.4, The Applicant submits below the names and
addresses of all outside contractors intended to be engaged by the
applicant on the temple's premises: —

Caterer: _____
         Name and Address   Phone No.

         Insured for: Workmen's Comp. (   ):
         Food Liability (   ):   Public Liability (   )

Decorator: _____
         Name and Address   Phone No.

         Insured for: Workmen's Comp. (   ):
         Public Liability (   )

Entertainers: _____
         Name and Address   Phone No.

         Insured for: Workmen's Comp. (   ):
         Public Liability (   )

Date: _____ SIGNATURE _____

Note: This form, with the required information supplied, MUST BE
FILED by the Applicant with the HOUSE COMMITTEE within
10 DAYS after filing of the Application.   (See Rule A.4)

Note: ALL CERTIFICATES OF INSURANCE COVERAGE, as indicated, MUST BE FILED by the Applicant with the HOUSE
COMMITTEE within 14 DAYS after filing of the application.
                                (See Rule A.5)

XI The Membership
Factor

HOW DO WE GET PEOPLE TO AFFILIATE WITH A SYNAGOGUE? HAVING become members of a synagogue, how do we go about getting them to attend worship services, adult education courses and social functions, etc.? How does a synagogue get its members to participate in the leadership and administrative aspects of its program? What can we do to keep families from dropping out when a boy becomes Bar Mitzvah or a girl is confirmed?

To arrive at the basic answers to these questions would require the assistance of psychologists and sociologists as well as philosophers. We would also have to involve Jewish historians and rabbis and delve deeply into the past and present of the Jewish people in our own country and in the many lands from which our forefathers came. For our purpose, however, it should be enough to assess the contemporary scene and to cite those positive and negative factors that lay and rabbinic leaders can readily utilize.

Members are the very lifeblood of the synagogue and those who would restrict the acquisition of new members risk making the contemporary synagogue stagnant. There must always be people bringing new ideas, new vitality, new purpose to the institution. There must always be families to replace those who drop out and, in our era of great mobility, to replace those who leave the community. These new people are assurance not only of the stability of the synagogue but added life, character, perspective, and the drive for greater and further accomplishment.

Since new members are desirable, we must ask ourselves where we will find the source, or, to paraphrase the Bible, "From whence cometh our help?" The following are the major sources:

1. *Religious Awakening* — Our generation has been witness to what some have labeled a religious revival of American Jewry. Whether or not this revival is real, there appears to be more emotional need to affiliate.

2. *Developing Neighborhood* — Shifting neighborhood patterns brought about by deterioration of urban areas and the movement to the suburbs.

3. *Education* — The desire of parents to have their children know about and understand their Jewish heritage and to partake in such religious experiences as Bar Mitzvah and Confirmation.

4. *Friends and Relatives* — They will be interested because their curiosity has been aroused.

5. *The Rabbi* — His role in the community, his sermons, the worship services he conducts, and his availability to perform ritual services at the great milestones of life — birth, marriage, and death — will attract many Jewish families.

6. *Social and Cultural* — Intellectual curiosity and the desire to identify with those of a similar heritage will stimulate many to consider synagogue affiliation.

Although there are these six positive factors, and you may be able to add an equal number which pertain to your local scene, we know that we cannot expect too many unaffiliated to make the first overtures. Thus, it is imperative that most congregations have an on-going program for the solicitation of new members. This program becomes the primary responsibility of the Membership Committee. Whether this committee be large or small, there are certain essential qualifications which each and every member of the committee should possess:

1. A deep commitment to Judaism, to his own synagogue, to the Jewish people of his own community, the nation and the world, and an ability to transmit this feeling to others.

2. A thorough knowledge of his own synagogue, its philosophy, program, goals, accomplishments, facilities, and its professional staff.

3. A personal involvement in many facets of the synagogue's worship, educational, fellowship, and administrative program.

Depending upon the size and age of the congregation, the Membership Committee may have few or many functions and it may be involved infrequently or be constantly at work. In any event, its major responsibilities are:

1. To create and organize recruitment drives.

2. To prepare and distribute materials that will make people aware of the synagogue and encourage affiliation.

3. To familiarize new members with the synagogue and orient them to its philosophy and program.

4. To integrate new members in such ways as will assure their active participation in synagogue life.

5. To determine and evaluate reasons for resignations.

While theoretical concepts may be helpful, the Membership Committee must eventually come to the point of actual recruitment. Techniques will vary from community to community and will be determined primarily on the basis of local conditions. Community Night, Welcome Sabbath, teas for the women, breakfasts and suppers for the men, open house at the religious school for the children, and a teen-age social — all these are standard recruitment techniques and when organized properly they produce results; for first you must meet and know the prospect before you can begin to suggest affiliation.

However, to make this recruitment effort truly effective we should be aware of some basic principles:

1. Recruitment is not a mass enterprise. Each person, each family is different and is motivated by different factors such as age, economic circumstances, occupation and educational level, special interests and skills, participation in other community activities, friends and associates.

2. Recruitment should be related to the committee member as well as the potential synagogue member. Neighbor should approach neighbor; those of similar profession or business should get together. Relate the background of your committee member to the information you possess on the prospect.

3. Recruitment is a face-to-face job. Brochures, letters, telephone calls all play a role in creating the interest, but the personal interview remains the most effective approach.

The first contact with the prospective member is of vital importance, for it may spell eventual success or failure. If nothing else, it is essential that the first interview, be it by telephone or face-to-face, be the source for creating the possibility of further contact. Hence, it is important that some information on the prospect be acquired and for this purpose the congregation should have a Prospective Members Card. This card may be brief or elaborate, but the following basic facts should be gathered:

1. The names of all adult members of the family, with address and telephone number.

2. The age of each adult.

3. The occupation, business address, and telephone.

4. The length of residence in the particular community.

5. Any previous synagogue affiliation and membership in other community organizations.

6. Relationship or acquaintance with members, the rabbi, or staff of the congregation, if any.

7. The names, ages, grades, and prior religious education of all children of the family.

8. The date, time, and place of the interview and who participated.

9. The name of the interviewer and adequate space for his comments, reactions, and suggestions for future action.

10. Recommendations of the Membership Committee.

In far too many instances the Membership Committee considers its job complete when it has secured the new member's signature on an application and received a check covering the monetary requirements. In reality, the work of the Membership Committee has just begun. One might very well say that the most important phase of its work still lies ahead. It is incumbent upon the Membership Committee to create a program that will convey to the new member the spirit of the congregation, to give him an understanding of its aims and aspirations, to familiarize him with the many facets of the synagogue's religious, educational, cultural, and social program, and to make him aware of his ties to the national movement and its institutions.

Whether consciously or unconsciously, a new member asks such questions as: What do I expect to derive from my membership? What part am I going to play in the life of the synagogue? What will the synagogue expect of me now that I am a member? To fail to make an attempt to answer these questions is to seriously weaken the fabric of the synagogue and to create problems for the future. Hence, it is vital that a thorough program for the orientation of new members be created and carried out. In many congregations this has taken the following form:

1. *A New Member Sabbath* — to introduce the newcomers to the religious aspects of the congregational program and to give them a sense of communal participation in worship and fellowship.

2. *A Meet-the-Rabbi Session* — to give them an opportunity to be greeted by the spiritual leader of the congregation and to hear from him and to have him answer questions on the basic tenets of Judaism and the ceremonial and ritual practices of the congregation.

3. *A Meet-the-Staff Session* — to present to the new members the professional staff of the congregation such as the educator or religious school principal, the synagogue administrator, the cantor or music director, the youth director, etc. Thus they become familiar with the many ramifications of the program and services offered by and through the congregation.

4. *Meet-the-Lay-Leaders Session* — to afford the new members an opportunity to become familiar with the individuals who guide the destinies of the congregation. This session should include an introduction to the administrative apparatus of the congregation, the Board and committee structure, as well as the role of the synagogue's affiliates.

This fourfold orientation program should serve as an effective base for the integration of the new member and give him the opportunity to answer at least two of the three questions previously cited. However, congregations frequently neglect answering the third, "What will the congregation expect of me?" One of the most frequent omissions falls into the area of financial obligation, for there is a tendency to feel that this is treacherous ground that should be avoided. Avoiding a frank and open discussion with new members about the financial situation of the synagogue only serves to create greater and more serious problems in the future.

A synagogue is a democratically run institution, and for a member to play his rightful role in a democracy he must know the facts. Knowing the facts, it can be anticipated that he will understand and be ready to assume his share of the financial obligations, present and future. A new member must also be made aware that an institution based on Jewish ethics and morals will always be conscious of his personal problems and that no one will be excluded from participation in synagogue life because of financial hardship.

They say that you can lead a horse to water but you can't make him drink. To translate this into synagogue parlance, one might say that you can sign up a new member, fully orient him to the program, but you can't always get him to participate in the life of the congregation. However, it is the sacred obligation of the congregation's lay as well as rabbinic and professional staff to bend every effort to make each member feel that he has an active association with some aspect of the synagogue's program.

To do this one must in reality develop and plan an individual activation program for each member-family and for each adult in that family. Because this job is of such great import and significance to the future of the congregation, you will find that many congregations have a separate and distinct Integration and Activation Committee. At the very least, there should be a subcommittee of the Membership Committee constantly concerned with this problem, for no one can derive true fulfilment from his synagogue association until he has had the opportunity to be associated with its different activities and programs.

The functions of the Integration and Activation Committee should encompass some of the following:

1. *Creating, and keeping up-to-date, a census of the member-families and individuals* — membership record cards and family folders are the essential tool. While these records will vary in size and format, they should include, in addition to the routine family background, this information:

   a. Educational background of all adult members of the family (both husband and wife) such as colleges attended, major courses of study, etc.

   b. Participation in other communal organizations and activities.

   c. Major interests, hobbies, and skills.

2. *Providing opportunities for participation* — encouraging new

members to join in the program of the synagogue based upon the information and knowledge garnered from the census record. Some congregations attempt to place each new member on at least one active committee.

3. *Recognition of talents and accomplishments of new members* — utilizing the census data to suggest to affiliates of the synagogue that they avail themselves of the skills, special abilities, and knowledge of new members so that they will be given responsibilities commensurate with their background and an early opportunity to demonstrable their leadership potentiality.

4. *Establishment of a roster system for service* — orientation, no matter how effective, will not always overcome the tendency to feel strange or ill at ease, nor will it always impart the sense of usefulness of the individual's contribution. Thus, at the outset it is wise to assign, on a rotating basis, certain tasks within the synagogue program.

The establishment of a roster system requires elaboration because of a common tendency for new members to feel a sense of exclusion. While this may not be a reality, we are aware that those who have been associated with a congregation for long periods tend to develop a proprietary interest in and feeling for their role and, consciously or subsconsciously, will resent sharing it. Yet, if we accept the postulate that it is important that new members be integrated and activated into the life of the synagogue so that they will develop a sense of belonging, we must provide a basis for such participation. It also presents the opportunity for a first emersion or "taste" of congregational life.

There are a few key areas where the roster system serves well:

1. *Ushering* — While this may be the responsibility of the Brotherhood in many congregations, by assigning one or two members to serve at one or more worship services during the congregational year, you introduce them to regular attendance at worship and to the fellowship of others serving the congregation.

2. *Hostess* — Hospitality and food service at the Oneg Shabbat or Social Hour, and at other social functions of the congregation is usually the function of the Sisterhood. However, inviting the newcomer to participate will quickly bring out the warmth and friendliness of the women of the congregation.

3. *Parking* — In some suburban congregations the committee handling parking renders an important service to the synagogue.

4. *Pulpit Participation* — Many synagogues ask members, old as well as new, to share the pulpit at worship services with officers, trustees, and rabbis, thus introducing them to a feeling of participating in this paramount aspect of the synagogue's existence.

While there are many techniques in locating, interesting, and activating new members, there must always be an understanding that the synagogue is a religious institution. In the words of Sam Weisberg, former executive director of Temple Emanu El, Cleveland, Ohio:

> There should be a minimum of distinction between older and newer families. There must always be prevalent the feeling that in the congregation the highest honors — service on the Board of Trustees, even elevation to the office of President — are obtainable by any deserving synagogue member. Vested interest has no place in congregational life. If the congregation and its spiritual leader are to serve the membership well, integration must be an on-going and all-embracing synagogue project. A membership campaign can only end successfully if there is satisfactory integration of the new recruits to the growing army of those already integrated, oriented, and activated.

REFERENCES

CROSSLAND, WELDON, *A Planned Program for the Church Year*, Abingdon Press, 1951.

Getting and Keeping Members, Adult Education Association of U.S.A.

Members Attitude Survey, UAHC, 1959.

PLEUTHNER, W. A., *Building Up Your Congregation*, Wilcox and Follet Co., 1951.

Procedure for Prospective Members, UAHC, 1961.

Twenty Questions — Why Temple Membership? UAHC, 1959.

WEISBERG, SAM, *Adding to Your Temple Membership*, UAHC, 1959.

SAMPLE MEMBERS' ATTITUDE SURVEY

The function of this survey is to determine, to the extent that statistical inquiry can do so, the degree of participation by the members of _____ in the activities which fulfil the purposes of this religious institution; the degree of satisfaction derived by those who do participate; the reasons for non-participation by those who do not; the strength and weaknesses of our congregational program as our members see them. The purpose of this inquiry shall be to formulate plans and programs for the strengthening of the bonds between our congregation and its members, based on the real needs of our members in their quest for a full and meaningful Jewish life. Responses will be made anonymously and no attempt at identification will be made.

Sabbath Services

1. How often, on the average, do you attend Friday evening services? _____ weekly, if possible; _____ twice monthly; _____ once a month; _____ a few times a year.

2. Please check the answers which most closely approximate your reaction to the services (not the sermon):

_____ Very satisfying religious experience
_____ Over-formal and cold
_____ Too much ritual
_____ *Union Prayerbook* stimulating and challenging
_____ Laymen should read part of service
_____ Satisfactory service
_____ Not enough congregational participation
_____ Warm congregational spirit and response
_____ Not enough ritual
_____ Unsatisfying and empty experience
_____ *Union Prayerbook* unstimulating and artificial
_____ *Union Prayerbook* adequate
_____ Laymen should read part of service routinely
_____ Sanctuary inspires greater religiosity
_____ Invisible choir adds to religious atmosphere
_____ I pray happily and feel closer to God
_____ Sanctuary helps to inhibit religiosity
_____ Invisible choir decreases response to service
_____ I find the atmosphere not conducive to concentrated prayer to God

3. What is your reaction to the musical portion of the services? _____ Excellent _____ Fair _____ Poor _____ Adequate congregational participation _____ Inadequate congregational participation _____ Too much traditional Jewish music _____ Not enough traditional Jewish music.

4. Please check the answer which most closely approximates your reaction to the post-service Oneg Shabbat:

a. _____ Very pleasant social hour and should be continued as is
b. _____ Very pleasant social hour but should be used occasionally for educational, cultural, musical and other programs
c. _____ Unsatisfactory social hour and should be abolished
d. _____ Should be used every Friday evening for some kind of serious programming as indicated in (b) above in addition to refreshments and socializing

5. How often do you attend Saturday morning services? _____ Whenever held _____ Occasionally _____ Only when invited by family of Bar Mitzvah _____ Never

6. Please check the answer which most closely approximates your reaction to the Bar Mitzvah service:

_____ Very satisfying religious experience
_____ Over-formal and cold
_____ Too much ritual
_____ *Union Prayerbook* stimulating and challenging
_____ Laymen should read part of service
_____ Satisfactory service
_____ Not enough congregational participation
_____ Warm congregational spirit and response
_____ Not enough ritual
_____ Unsatisfying and empty experience
_____ *Union Prayerbook* unstimulating and artificial
_____ *Union Prayerbook* adequate
_____ Laymen should read part of service routinely
_____ Sanctuary inspires greater religiosity
_____ Invisible choir adds to religious atmosphere
_____ I pray happily and feel closer to God
_____ Sanctuary helps to inhibit religiosity
_____ Invisible choir decreases response to service
_____ I find the atmosphere not conducive to concentrated prayer to God

7. How often, on the average, do you attend services on Passover, Sukos, and other holidays, except Confirmation and the High Holy Days?____ Regularly, if possible _____ Sometimes _____ Almost never _____ Never

8. If you attend High Holy Day services, please check the answers which include your reactions to them.

   IN THE SANCTUARY:

   _____ Completely fulfiling of the purposes of the High Holy Days
   _____ Totally unfulfiling of the purposes of the High Holy Days
   _____ Adequate, but not exceptional
   _____ Less than adequate, but bearable

   IN THE AUDITORIUM:

   _____ Completely fulfiling of the purposes of the High Holy Days
   _____ Totally unfulfiling of the purposes of the High Holy Days
   _____ Adequate, but not exceptional
   _____ Less than adequate, but bearable
   _____ Adequate except for piped-in sermon
   _____ Other arrangement for sermon essential

9. If you have a child or children in the religious school, what is your general feeling about the quality of our school?_____ Excellent _____ Good _____ Fair _____ Mediocre _____ Poor

10. When your children bring information about ceremonies and home practices from the school, what is your reaction?

    _____ Introduce them in our home if we don't already observe them
    _____ Listen to them and try them out if we like them or feel like it
    _____ Listen to them but rarely observe any
    _____ Listen to them but never observe any
    _____ Resent the school for attempting to propagandize my home

11. Please check those observances you routinely carry on in your home:

    _____ Motzi before meals
    _____ Bedtime prayer
    _____ Light candles on Shabos and holidays
    _____ Recite or sing Kiddush on Shabos and holidays
    _____ Light Chanuko candles each night
    _____ Seder at home or with family

_____Some kind of Purim observance
_____Some kind of service for Rosh Ha-shono eve
_____Some kind of Sukos observance
_____ Some kind of Shovuos observance

12. To what extent do you participate in the adult education program of the congregation? (Includes Sisterhood and Men's Club sponsored classes)

_____ Attend every possible class _____ Attend frequently_____ Attend occasionally_____ Attend none

Would you attend more often if your business and household duties permitted?_____Yes _____No, I'm not interested

13. FOR WIVES ONLY: To what extent do you participate in the work of the Sisterhood?

_____Very active and derive satisfaction from activity
_____Fairly active and derive satisfaction
_____Fairly active but only out of sense of duty
_____Attend meetings frequently but take no other responsibility
_____Attend meetings occasionally but take no other responsibility
_____Never attend meetings and take no responsibility

If you are not active and do not attend meetings frequently, please check your reasons, in addition to lack of time:

_____Meetings are dull   _____Too much fund-raising
_____Meetings are too formal   activity
_____Ladies are unfriendly   _____Meetings are too in-
_____Too much Judaism in   formal
        program   _____Not enough substance
_____ Programs too   in program
        superficial   _____ Too expensive
                                        _____ Program too deep

14. FOR HUSBANDS ONLY: To what extent do you participate in the work of the Men's Club?

_____ Very active and derive satisfaction from activity
_____ Fairly active and derive satisfaction
_____ Fairly active but only out of sense of duty
_____ Attend meetings frequently but take no other responsibility
_____Attend meetings occasionally but take no other responsibility
_____ Never attend meetings and take no responsibility

If you are not active and do not attend meetings frequently, please check your reasons, in addition to lack of time:

_____ Meetings are dull   _____ Too much fund-raising
_____ Meetings are too formal   activity
_____ Men are unfriendly   _____Meetings are too in-
_____Too much Judaism in   formal
        program   _____Not enough substance
_____Programs too   in program
        superficial˘   _____ Too expensive
                                        _____ Programs too deep

15. FOR YOUNGER FAMILIES ONLY: To what extent do you participate in the work of the Wedding Band?

_____Very active and derive satisfaction from activity
_____Fairly active and derive satisfaction

_____Fairly active but only out of sense of duty
_____Attend meetings frequently but take no other responsibility
_____Attend meetings occasionally but take no other responsibility
_____ Never attend meetings and take no responsibility

If you are not active and do not attend meetings frequently, please check your reasons, in addition to lack of time:

_____Meetings are dull   _____Too much fund-raising
_____Meetings are too formal   _____Meetings are too informal
_____People are unfriendly   _____Not enough substance in program
_____Too much Judaism in program _____ Programs too deep
_____Programs too superficial   _____Too expensive

16. If you have teen-age children, to what extent are they active in our temple youth program?

_____Very active and derive satisfaction from activity
_____Fairly active and derive satisfaction
_____Fairly active but only out of sense of duty
_____Attend meetings frequently but take no other responsibility
_____Attend meetings occasionally but take no other responsibility
_____Never attend meetings and take no responsibility

What is your reaction to the content of the youth program?

_____ Excellent as is
_____ Too much Jewish content now
_____ Not enough Jewish content now

17. If you are a member of a congregational committee, please check the answers closest to your reaction:

a. _____Worthwhile investment b. _____ Committee has too much responsi-
     of time   bility
_____A duty, so I perform it   _____Committee functions well
_____A waste of my time   _____ Committee does not have enough
                                responsibility

18. If you are not a member of a congregational committee, check your reasons for not becoming involved:

_____Interested, but no time _____Not interested in synagogue except for children and/or services, etc. _____ Have time and am interested, but do not feel welcome because small group controls all activities_____Lazy _____ Other (Please specify)

19. Please check the phrase which most closely approximates your feeling about _____ .

_____I'm proud to be a member and _____ is important in my life
_____ I joined for the sake of my children and I'm satisfied so long as you leave me alone
_____ I'm not happy with _____ at present and wish a lot of improvements could be made

20. Have you a desire to be active or more active in the activities of _____ _____Yes _____No. Have you been fully afforded the opportunity to be active or more active?_____Yes_____ No.

21. Do you feel that exclusive of your ideas you are contributing financially the most that you could reasonably afford, to the support of _____ ?

22. Is the amount of your financial support determined ____in whole____in part____not at all, by the extent of your interest in the synagogue as a whole? Is it determined solely by the:

a. extent of your interest in the religious services _____ Yes _____No.

b. extent of your interest in _____ Men's Club _____ Sisterhood _____ in other activities

c. your financial ability to contribute

d. Would greater participation by you in the affairs and activities of the synagogue bring you closer to and increase your interests in the synagogue _____Yes _____No.

23. Might such an increased interest on your part in the synagogue result in increased financial support _____ Yes _____ No.

24. So that the Survey Committee can effectively evaluate the answers, will you please indicate your yearly average contributions to the synagogue in the last two years (exclusive of dues). If you were a member for less than two years, so indicate, and answer the questions based upon total contributions, exclusive of dues   None _____; $1 to $24 _____; $25 to $49 _____; $50 to $74 _____; $75 to $99 _____; $100 to $149 _____; $150 to $199 _____; $200 to $299 _____; $300 to $399 _____; $400 to $499 _____; $500 to $999 _____; $1000 to $1999 _____; $2000 to $2999 _____; $3000 or more _____.

25. a. If, in accordance with our Jewish heritage and tradition, your synagogue activities were more closely related to your daily living and concern with current social and ethical problems of the community, would the synagogue be more meaningful for you _____Yes _____No.

b. Under such circumstances, might you be inclined to participate to a greater extent in the activities of the synagogue _____ Yes _____ No.

26. Do you read the congregational bulletin?

27. Do you want public Kol Nidrei night appeal for funds?

28. Do you attend congregational meetings?

29. Would you like more congregational meetings?

30. How long have you been a member of_____ ? _____Years

31. Including above period, how long have you been a member of a synagogue? _____ Years

32. If you were not raised in the branch of Judaism with which this synagogue is affiliated, what was your previous status?_____ Conservative _____Orthodox _____ Reform _____Nothing as adult.

33. Please add any comments, suggestions, opinions, or ideas which you feel will help the Survey Committee in reaching conclusions of maximum value to you and to the other members of our congregation.

FORM FOR NEIGHBORHOOD SURVEY

Name (husband & wife)_____

Address_____Telephone_____

Children _____

_____

Are you presently affiliated with a synagogue?_____

_____

Would you like a conducted tour of our temple?_____

Would you like to be invited to:

        Men's Club Meeting_____

        Sisterhood Meeting_____

        Couples Club Meeting_____

        Youth Group Meeting _____

_____

Canvasser's comments

    Should family be invited to join?_____

    What follow up is necessary?_____

    Other observations for guidance of Membership Committee

_____

_____

_____

_____

_____

                                           Canvasser

SAMPLE PRE-APPLICATION FORM

Suggested Interview Appointment

_____

_____

_____

Name_____Date of Birth _____

Wife's Maiden Name _____ Date of Birth _____

Residence_____ Zone ____Phone _____

Occupation _____ Firm Name _____

Business Address _____ Zone ____Phone _____

How long have you lived in the community?_____

Previous congregation affiliation (if any)_____

If you know any members of the temple, please list their names

_____

_____

_____

Unmarried children (of all ages) in household:

NAME	DATE OF BIRTH	GRADE IN SCHOOL
_____	_____	_____
_____	_____	_____
_____	_____	_____
_____	_____	_____
_____	_____	_____

Date of Inquiry _____.

SAMPLE MEMBERSHIP APPLICATION FORM

_____ 195_____

I hereby apply for membership in_____ and agree, if accepted, to pay annual dues as fixed by the Board of Trustees.

The following information is listed for consideration by the Board:

Name_____ Date of Birth_____

Wife's Maiden Name _____ Date of Birth _____

Residence_____Zone____Phone _____

Occupation_____ Firm Name_____

Business Address_____ Zone____ Phone _____

Previous Affiliation (if any) _____

Sponsors _____

_____

Signed

The following is the reverse side of membership application form above.

I have these unmarried children (of all ages) in my household:

Name	Date of Birth	School and Grade
_____	_____	_____
_____	_____	_____
_____	_____	_____

Others living with me are:

Name	Age	Married?	Relationship	Congregational Affiliation
_____	____	____	_____	_____
_____	____	____	_____	_____

My married children are:

	Address	Congregation
_____	_____	_____
_____	_____	_____

My family is interested in serving_____ in the following:

☐ Membership ☐ Cemetery ☐ Building Fund ☐ Youth Leadership
☐ Fellowship and Hospitality ☐ Ushering ☐ Music ☐ Ritual
☐ Religious School ☐ Teaching ☐ Photography ☐ Publicity
☐ Art Work ☐ Bulletin ☐ Secretarial Assistance ☐ Adult Programs
☐ Friday Evening Programs ☐ Talent Group ☐ _____Singers

TEMPLE BETH EL of NORTHERN VALLEY
Congregational Census

PLEASE DO NOT WRITE IN THIS SPACE

No. _____ 1 - 5

Class _____ 78
_____ 79
_____ 80

CARD ONE — • BASIC FAMILY DATA AND DATES

6-20 NAME

21-34 ADDRESS

21-23 NUMBER   24-33 STREET   34 TOWN

35-41 PHONE

42-43 Month 44-45 Day 46-47 Year 48-49 YEAR JOINED TEMPLE

42-47 DATE OF MARRIAGE

50-64 PREVIOUS CONGREGATIONAL AFFILIATION

65-74 Name of Congregation   City

75-76 Year   (Check One) 77
1 Reform   2 Conserv   3 Ortho

ONE CARD FOR EACH LINE COMPLETED (Dup.1-41) — • VITAL STATISTICS

FAMILY RELATIONSHIP	42 CODE	NAME 43-52 FIRST	53 Initial	54 SEX	DATE OF BIRTH 55-56 Month	57-58 Day	59-60 Year	SECULAR EDUCATION 61-62 Last Grade Completed	63 Degree	64-65 Major if College	RELIGIOUS EDUCATION 66-67 No of Years	68 Type *	69-1 Bar Mitz	69-2 Conf	70 Emphasis **
HUSBAND	1			M											
WIFE	2			F											
CHILD	3														
CHILD	3														
CHILD	3														
CHILD	3														
CHILD	3														
Other *	4														
Other *	4														

*Please specify relationship

* Daily or Weekly   ** Hebrew-Religion, etc.

ONE CARD FOR EACH LINE COMPLETED (Dup.1-41) — • YAHRZEITS

FAMILY RELATIONSHIP	42 CODE	NAME 43-57 LAST	58-69 FIRST and INITIAL	DATE OF DEATH 70-71 Month	72-73 Day	74-75 Year
Husband Mother	5					
Husband Father	6					
Wife Mother	5					
Wife Father	6					
HUSBAND	1					
WIFE	2					
* OTHER						

Please check one below to be observed on Anniversary according to:

76 ☐ Jewish Calendar   ☐ Secular Calendar

TEMPLE BETH EL of NORTHERN VALLEY
Congregational Census

• OCCUPATION AND INDUSTRY

42	OCCUPATION			EMPLOYED BY		
Code	CODE 43-52	TITLE 53-67	NAME	ADDRESS 68-77	CITY 78	KIND OF BUSINESS 79-80
HUSBAND	A					
WIFE	B					
OTHER *						

*Please specify

• TEMPLE INTERESTS AND ACTIVITIES

	Col.	H	W	O*		Col.	H	W	O
RITUAL	43				GIRL SCOUTS	53			
REL SCHOOL	44				INTERFAITH ACTIVITIES	54			
YOUTH ACTIVITIES	45				HOUSE & GROUNDS	55			
WELFARE	46				FACILITIES PLANNING	56			
SOCIAL ACTION	47				ADULT EDUCATION	57			
MEMBERSHIP	48								
MEMBERSHIP MAINTENANCE	49								
CEMETERY	50								
LIBRARY	51								
BOY SCOUTS	52								

* Other Adult - please specify

XII Public Relations
and Publicity

A RELIGIOUS INSTITUTION CANNOT SERVE ITS MEMBERS AND THE COM-
munity if it does not have public support or at least public ac-
ceptance. Synagogues have come to the realization that public
relations and publicity play a vital role in their stability and prosperity. Every institution projects an image to the public and it
is essential that the synagogue know what image it is creating in
the eyes of its members and the community, Jewish as well as non-
Jewish.

It is important that we understand at the outset the meaning
of the term "public relations." A public relations program is no
substitute for a Jewishly meaningful program in the synagogue.
Further, in the words of Kalman Druck, of Harshe, Rotman and
Druck, Inc., and chairman of the UAHC's Public Relations Advisory Committee:

> Public relations need not mean Madison Avenue techniques,
> slick prose and glossy art work, half-truths and high pres-
> sure. Public relations, rather, can mean exactly what the
> term would seem to imply — maintaining relations — better,
> more meaningful relations with the public.

The first step in a sound synagogue public relations program is
the creation of a good committee. If you were to decide on a
committee of six people, the UAHC's Public Relations Department recommends that they be chosen on the following basis:

1. A veteran synagogue member who knows the history and
traditions of the congregation and therefore brings a sense of
perspective to the program.

2. A Trustee with a sound knowledge of the property, the program, and the administration of the synagogue.

3. One with special skills — newspaper reporter, advertising
executive, professional photographer, artist, etc.

4. A knowledgeable person in the area of television and/or radio.

5. A member with ideas, drive, and exuberance.

157

6. As chairman, a person with leadership qualities, common sense, and some background or acquaintance with public relations.

There is one caution worth noting — an apathetic professional, one with little or no commitment to the importance of the synagogue program, will generally prove to be of little use. The person with belief plus enthusiasm will prove to be of great value.

The Objectives

What are the objectives of the committee? We must know these before we can consider the role it shall play. The objectives might include the following:

1. To keep the membership informed of the synagogue program.

2. To make the synagogue a more inviting place.

3. To create interest in the synagogue among the Jewish and general community.

4. To project the character and accomplishments of the synagogue, Judaism, and the Jewish people.

5. To initiate and develop special events within the congregation.

6. To create the atmosphere which will encourage affiliation with the congregation and activate those already affiliated.

The Synagogue Bulletin

One of the most frequent and effective contacts with the membership is through the synagogue bulletin. It is a reflection of the synagogue's program and progress. It serves to inform the membership, but in addition it should serve the following functions:

1. Educate and Instruct

2. Inspire

3. Remind

4. Amuse

Each issue of the synagogue bulletin should contain the following basic essentials:

1. *Latest News* — a new program or lecture series, progress in the building campaign, newsworthy accomplishments of members and staff, etc.

2. *Editorials* — forthright opinions on issues affecting the synagogue, the Jewish people, or Jewish ideals and ethics; the rabbi's column, messages from officers, professional staff, and lay leaders regarding the synagogue program and the members' responsibilities.

3. *Special Features* — columns devoted to the programs of the auxiliaries and special activities of the synagogue, as well as the national institutions with which the congregation is affiliated.

4. *Acknowledgments* — expressing appreciation for contributions and assistance, human interest stories about the members and their families, etc.

While the rabbi and/or synagogue administrator frequently assume responsibility for the entire bulletin, it is highly desirable that there be an editorial staff and volunteer reporters from the membership covering every facet of synagogue life.

Direct Mail

The cost of mailing letters or flyers has become one of the major expenses of the contemporary synagogue and it is, therefore, essential that this vital contact and form of information be used effectively. The printed word or the typed letter can be an effective tool of the synagogue's public relations program, but more frequently it calls forth objections of "too much" or fails to attract attention and ends up in the waste basket.

A letter or flyer should use as few words as possible and still get the message across. It should have one message, not several. Letterheads, invitations, folders, and brochures should contain a basic symbol or design that represents to your reader the congregation. At all times it should be esthetically pleasing.

The Press

The local newspapers and the Anglo-Jewish weekly in your community represent the most direct route to the public. What you must have and what the press wants is NEWS. If any aspect of your synagogue program or its membership represent real news, the religious editors of the press will be happy to utilize it. The story must be presented clearly and economically — with a minimum of words and without exaggerating and editorializing.

Newspaper people are busy people who work against continuous deadlines. Develop a contact with the person who handles religious news and find out his routine requirements schedules, and then abide by them.

Outside Resources

Large congregations may find it possible or necessary to engage a professional public relations consultant or firm, either on a retainer or part-time basis. Such a professional should be responsible to the Public Relations Committee in regard to policies and practices.

When something occurs in your synagogue or your community which is unusual, colorful, or experimental, and you think that other congregations and communities should be made aware of it, remember that your congregation belongs to a national movement. Contact the public relations department of your national organization for advice and assistance. Always keep in mind that even if a story does not seem to have national significance it may be of interest to the surrounding communities. Bear in mind that there is a regional office in your area and it can do a more effective job in publicizing plans and programs that go beyond the confines of the individual congregation or community.

Your public relations program should be a two-way street. Your committee should always keep an eye on what is being done by other congregations and the national institutions with which you are affiliated. For instance, the many-faceted program of the UAHC, with its departments and programs serving the Reform movement in the fields of education, social action, youth, temple administration, interfaith activity, and congregations in foreign lands, will frequently provide exciting material for your synagoue bulletin as well as the local press, radio, and TV.

"The Little Things"

No matter the extent of the public relations effort of the synagogue, we must not forget that frequently it is the "little things" that prove important. Our members and the public may not judge the synagogue on the size and beauty of its sanctuary or the names and numbers of prominent lecturers on the synagogue program, but on their personal contact with the synagogue and its membership. Because of this important factor, Max D. Weinless, executive director of Congregation Shaare Torah of Brooklyn, New York, defines public relations as follows:

> I have seen dozens of definitions of public relations. The one I like best is "the art of making friends and getting people to participate". . . . I firmly believe in the principle of telling your story to your people, be it a budget problem, a fund-raising effort, a membership campaign, etc. Knowing the problems and the facts, they will often bend every effort to help solve them.
>
> People may not understand the workings of the synagogue — they resent what they consider the "inner clique" — the workers — the "do-gooders." They may often complain about the cost of the synagogue program, the method of raising funds, etc. We must, therefore, constantly bring to the attention of our members and the community our services in all areas, however extensive they may be. All of us respect "service to the community" and will go a long way to maintain this service and often want to help expand it.

It is important that the Public Relations Committee do a frequent self-analysis of how the synagogue rates in the "little things" that seem to be so important in the eyes, the mind, and the heart of the average person. Mr. Weinless provides us with the following basic check list:

1. Are the entrances to your facilities clean and inviting?
2. Landscaping neat and trim?
3. Is your building clean, well-lighted, and ventilated?
4. Do your ushers extend a proper welcome at services?
5. Are there adequate prayer books, etc.?
6. Are office visitors welcomed pleasantly?
7. Is the reception room attractive?
8. Are individual needs handled efficiently?
9. Do the people working at the synagogue seem happy?
10. Is the telephone answered courteously?
11. Is your catering department making friends?
12. Are requests to return telephone calls handled promptly?
13. Is correspondence answered or acknowledged with minimum delay?
14. Do letters, brochures, publications, etc., show thought and thorough preparation?
15. Do thank-you notes go regularly to people for their good work?
16. Do we take proper cognizance of our members who have achieved public recognition?
17. Do committee members say they enjoy their meetings?
18. Do meetings start and end on time?
19. Is your youth, adult education program, etc., effective?
20. Is your school good?

Mr. Weinless agrees that one could add an equal number of criteria to the list, but more important than the number of criteria is how your program measures up to the criteria.

The real meaning of public relations to the future of your synagogue might well be summed up in the words of Mr. Kalman Druck:

> Like charity, a good public relations program should begin at home. It should start with the membership of your congregation or, even before that, with your own Board of Trustees. Properly used, public relations can help your temple, Judaism, the Jewish community in your locale, and Jews as people to be properly respected, appreciated, and understood. In a sense, everything that happens in your congrega-

tion is bound up in some measure with the public relations picture you will create.

REFERENCES

Effective Public Relations, Adult Education Association of the U.S.A.

FINE, BENJAMIN, *Educational Publicity,* Harper & Bros., 1951.

Manual for Synagogue Bulletin Editors, United Synagogue of America, 1960.

Public Relations Kit, UAHC, 1961.

STUBER, STANLEY I., *Public Relations Manual for Churches,* Doubleday & Co., 1951.

XIII The Congregational Cemetery

Historical Background

NEARLY FOUR THOUSAND YEARS AGO ABRAHAM PURCHASED THE Cave of Machpelah from the Hittites in Hebron to be used as a burial site for his wife, Sarah. The progenitor of our faith, who fathered the concept of one God and thereby laid the basis of belief in the inalienable rights of man and brotherly love, is also the father of our concept of burial and memorialization.

It must be emphasized that Abraham *purchased* the land, rather than accepted it as a gift, because he wanted to guarantee its Jewish character permanently.

Ground interment has been an eternal custom with the Jew because burial was commanded in the Torah: "Return unto the ground . . . for dust thou art, and unto dust shalt thou return" (Genesis 3:19). The ancient Hebrews regarded interment as being "gathered unto his people" (Genesis 49:33; Numbers 27:13), or as "slept with his fathers" (I Kings 2:10; 14:31).

In the Middle Ages the Jewish cemetery was known as *Bes Chayim* (House of Life) and *Bes Olom* (Everlasting Abode). It was kept beautiful with shrubs and trees, which led the Christians to call it *Hortus Judeorium* (Gardens of the Jews).

Jews consider the last resting place of their departed to be hallowed ground. We deem it a matter of reverence, honor, and basic Jewish respect to give scrupulous attention to the requirements of Jewish customs and traditions as to where we lay our departed to final repose. The purchase of land for interment purposes must have an assurance of and unassailable right of perpetuity. An atmosphere of serenity and beauty, blending a modern and an ancestral spirit, provides for the repose of the dead and for the consolation of the living.

We consider the act of burial a deed of righteousness or, better yet, an act of lovingkindness, a *mitzvah*. It is an obligation upon the next of kin, and after them on all humanity, to bury the body

164

of man in dignity. The body is the receptacle, created by God to contain within it the "image of God." Being the creation of God, the image of man, the body, must never be placed in a position of indignity. We must not desecrate the dignity of man. Therefore, even though the spirit has departed, the receptacle must be treated with dignity and respect, for it is the creation of God, the mantle for the "breath of life."

In the United States the acquisition of a burial ground was often the first act performed by the handful of Jews residing in a community. Many of the early congregations and fraternal organizations originated as small groups to provide proper burial for members. We still have a few Jewish cemeteries that date back to Revolutionary days.

Establishing a Cemetery

One of the signs of maturity of any Jewish congregation is ownership of a suitable cemetery. It is one of the most important and personal phases of the congregation's religious program. The cemetery is one of the important adjuncts of the synagogue and many people will join a congregation because of this important facility. The cemetery also has great sentimental value from the standpoint of attachment of families to the congregation because their dear departed are interred in the congregational cemetery. In many congregations the cemetery is also a source of considerable income to the congregation. During the depression of the 1930's, many a cemetery proved to be a "life-saver" to the synagogue when the congregational treasury was at a low ebb.

The congregational cemetery has a twofold function in the community. It must provide a permanent and sacred resting place for those who have gone before and it must also become a source of consolation to the living. It reflects the culture and concern of the congregation.

On acquiring cemetery property, the congregation should strive to obtain a parcel of land of sufficient acreage to assure a lengthy and continual service to the members and the community. Special attention should be given to whether or not the cemetery is to be located in an unincorporated area or an incorporated area. Once the land is purchased, it should immediately be dedicated in its entirety for cemetery and burial purposes *only*. This will assure the congregation that the cemetery will be tax free, so long as they do not rent or lease portions thereof for any purpose. Any renting or leasing of land in the cemetery immediately makes that portion taxable by the city or county in which the land is located.

The purchase by the congregation of cemetery property is only the beginning as far as outlay of money is concerned. Today it is practically impossible to start a new cemetery unless substantial funds are available, or can be borrowed. Such major items as plotting and layout of sections, landscaping, water supply, roads, caretaker's quarters, trucks, equipment, maintenance help, etc., must be considered before the first interment space can be sold.

More than 90 per cent of the new cemeteries today are of the garden or memorial park type. The old graveyard is fast becoming a thing of the past. The object of the memorial park cemetery is to create a beautiful garden-type park which is an inspiration to behold. It eliminates the crowded headstones standing row upon row and it avoids competition of expensive monuments. In place of headstones, dignified and uniform bronze or granite markers are placed on the resting places of loved ones amid those quiet beauties of nature in which so many find comfort in time of sorrow. These memorial parks have done away with the curbs, the fences, and varieties of statuary. In their place are stately shade trees, rolling lawns, fountains, and growing flowers where one can relive cherished memories of relatives and friends. The turn toward garden cemeteries goes on at an accelerated pace and many monument cemeteries have opened new sections with bronze or granite marker memorials.

With the development of memorial parks has come the practice of establishing and building a trust fund (Perpetual Care Fund or Endowment Care Fund) to assure the permanent and proper maintenance of the resting places of our beloved departed, and to give the cemetery grounds their proper and fitting appearance. The beauty of the modern cemetery and the satisfaction that the burial estate will be maintained for years to come without additional cost have increased the demand for burial property in advance of need. The responsibility of the modern cemetery does not begin and end with the sale of a piece of ground, plus its maintenance and technical details of interment; its responsibility extends to the living as well as service for the dead.

In launching a new cemetery, therefore, consideration must be given to the establishment of a Perpetual Care Fund, i.e., the setting aside of a certain percentage of the proceeds of the sale of each burial plot into a special trust fund. The principal of this fund is subject to the laws of each state and the income is used exclusively for the maintenance of the cemetery.

It must also be pointed out that the entire operation of the congregational cemetery must conform to all city, county, and state laws.

In communities where land for cemetery purposes is not available, and in the case of the smaller congregations, a feasible and beneficial solution to acquiring burial facilities is either to purchase outright or to reserve for their exclusive use a section of land in an established cemetery.

Cemetery property and space can be divided into three separate and distinct parts:

1. Ground Burial Space
   a. Single Interment spaces
   b. Companion plots (2 interment spaces for husband and wife)
   c. Family plots (3 or more interment spaces together)
      Note: Depending upon division and landscaping of grounds, one acre will generally provide between 750 and 1100 interment spaces.
2. Mausoleum Crypts for Above-Ground Entombment
3. Niches in Mausoleum and/or Columbarium for Inurnment of Cremated Remains. (On the West Coast, where cremation is prevalent among liberal Jews, the cemetery usually operates its own crematory for the incineration of the remains.)

Administration of Cemetery

The administration of the congregational cemetery, as a spiritual function of the synagogue, should be approached from the following viewpoints:

1. An essential service to the congregants in times of bereavement.

2. A businesslike operation, the income from which, allowing for the portion allocable to the Perpetual Care Fund, will properly maintain the cemetery property, and any surplus from operations can be used to further the general program of the congregation.

The management and control of the congregational cemetery should be vested in the Board of Trustees, which may delegate some or all of its cemetery powers to a Cemetery Committee. The chairman and members of this committee should be appointed by the president, subject to the approval of the Board of Trustees. The Cemetery Committee should be composed of the caliber of congregants in whom the general membership reposes the utmost confidence.

The Cemetery Committee usually exercises such powers and performs such functions and duties with regard to the management of the cemetery property and funds as the Board of Trustees delegates to it from time to time, consistent with the congregation's by-laws. In such connection, and subject to the approval of the Board, the Cemetery Commitee usually promulgates rules and regulations for the conduct of its affairs.

All funds and receipts derived from the sale of burial sites and other aspects of the operation and management of the cemetery are the property of the congregation. These monies should be segregated and be accounted for separately from other congregational assets and income. Investments and disbursements therefrom should be made by the Board of Trustees, or such officers or members of the Cemetery Committee as may be designated by it.

It is recommended that the chairman of the Cemetery Committee be selected from the Board of Trustees. In a number of congregations there is a by-law provision to the effect that the chairman of the Cemetery Committee serves as an ex-officio member of the Board, with all the rights and privileges of an elected member of the Board.

The chairman of the Cemetery Committee should render regular reports to the Board regarding the operations, finances, and services of the cemetery.

It is recommended that the entire Board of Trustees and the full Cemetery Committee meet at least once a year at the cemetery for a general inspection.

The management of the cemetery should be centered in the synagogue office, under the direction of the synagogue's executive director, or a duly designated assistant to the executive director, who shall be responsible to the Cemetery Committee and the Board. In smaller congregations this task usually devolves upon the chairman of the Cemetery Committee.

The physical operation of the cemetery should be under the direction of a capable cemetery superintendent or caretaker who should be responsible to the chairman of the Cemetery Committee and the executive director.

Rules and Regulations

One of the most important documents that a cemetery needs is adequate rules and regulations which are reasonable and which are uniformly applied to everyone. These rules and regulations must cover all of the rights and functions of the cemetery and they must protect the cemetery, the lot owners, the general public, and any other person concerned. These rules and regulations should be accurate and precise and fully explained (and a copy mailed) to every lot owner at the time of the original sale. In this manner, future confusion and difficulties will be avoided. It is essential that the rules and regulations provide a method by which they can be revised and kept up to date. The Cemetery Committee should study these rules regularly to make certain that they provide for all contingencies.

Records and Forms

The importance of a proper system of records in a cemetery cannot be overemphasized. The basic records are of more importance than in almost any other enterprise. In business, when property of any kind is sold, little reference to the transaction is necessary and record of the transaction need not be kept for any length of time. In the case of a cemetery, however, it is necessary that the records shall be not only correct and complete, but *permanent*. Instead of interest ceasing when the lot is sold, it is only after a sale is made that the most important entries are required, for it is then that interments occur and the entries regarding these must be detailed and accurate. They may extend over a period of years and reference to them may be made by future generations. Even after all interments have been made, the records must be preserved indefinitely for reasons based on the demands of law and of sentiment.

The following is a suggested classification of congregational cemetery records:

A. Sales

B. Operational

C. Financial

D. Minutes of Cemetery Committee

The usual records are:

Name of form	*Description*
A. Sales Record	
1. Sales Invoice	Pre-numbered. Original to purchaser, duplicate to lot owner's envelope, triplicate to bookkeeper.
2. Certificate of Ownership	Pre-numbered. Original to purchaser, duplicate to lot owner's envelope.
3. Receipt for Certificate of Ownership	
4. Contract of purchase (for installment sale)	Original to purchaser. Duplicate to lot owner's envelope.

Name of form	*Description*
5. Installment sale promissory note	
6. Annual Flower Planting Card	Original to be kept in synagogue office. File alphabetically. Duplicate to cemetery office. File alphabetically. Show name of deceased, lot owner, payee, date paid, letters sent.
7. Annual Winter Blanket Card	Same as A-6.

B. Operational Records

1. Lot Record	Card, size 5x8, for synagogue office — white; same for cemetery office — canary. File numerically.
2. Lot owner's envelope and layout	Size approximately 8x11 to fit standard file cabinet. File alphabetically.
3. Lot owner's record (punched for binder)	Same as face of lot owner's envelope. To be filed alphabetically at cemetery office.
4. Application for interment	Detailed information blank.
5. Lot owner's authorization	Pad, size 5x8. File in lot owner's envelope.
6. Interment Permit	Original to cemetery caretaker; duplicate to lot owner's envelope. Pad, size 5x8.
7. Interment Record	Pre-numbered. Punched for binder. Original to be kept at synagogue office. File alphabetically by name of deceased. Duplicate to be filed in lot owner's envelope. Triplicate to cemetery office. File alphabetically by name of deceased. Quadruplicate to be kept at synagogue office. File numerically.

Name of form	*Description*
8. Cemetery Daily Interment Book	Show date of interment, name of deceased, section number, lot number, interment space number, interment record number.
9. Application for marker foundation	Original to monument firm, duplicate to cemetery caretaker, triplicate to be filed in lot owner's envelope.
10. Receipt for foundation fee	Use regular numbered receipt book. Original to monument firm, duplicate remains in receipt book.
11. Future interment authorization	File in lot owner's envelope.
12. Heirship affidavit	File in lot owner's envelope.
13. Disinterment authorization	File in lot owner's envelope.
14. Current lot price list and various cemetery charges	
15. Plat	Showing lots and areas, water system, drainage system.
16. Wall map	
17. Customer's map	Miniature of wall map.
18. Equipment record	

C. Financial Records
  1. Cash Receipts Journal
  2. Check Register
  3. Accounts Receivable Ledger and Index
  4. Charge Journal
  5. General Ledger and Tabs
  6. Collection Tickler
  7. Purchase Orders
  8. Payroll Time Book
  9. Payroll Report
  10. Statement

11. Receipt Book
12. Investment Record
13. Insurance Record
14. Financial Reports

Many of the records cited are illustrated in the booklet *Cemetery Operations and Procedures* (UAHC-NATA Synagogue Research Survey #5), published by the Union of American Hebrew Congregations. Remington Rand, Royal McBee, and other companies have devised excellent cemetery records. It should be emphasized that all cemetery records should be kept in fireproof (not fire-resistant) cabinets.

It must also be pointed out that an audit of the books should be made at least annually by a professional accountant.

The Cemetery Committee is one of the most important committees in a congregation. It should meet regularly and keep an accurate record of its proceedings. Its minutes should be kept in a standard corporation, hard-cover, pre-numbered, good quality paper minute book.

Stimulating Pre-Need Sales

The following publicity media can be used advantageously to promote pre-need sales in a congregational cemetery:
  A. Direct mail
     1. Letters
     2. Printed brochure
  B. Synagogue bulletin notices and display ads
  C. Ads in Anglo-Jewish weeklies

The following are illustrations of letters which have proved effective:

Illustration A

Within the next few moments you will make a decision. You *may* decide to fill out and mail the enclosed card now or you may decide to wait until another "tomorrow."

Dear Friends,

The hallowed ground that is Beth El Memorial Park is today a place of serene beauty. Time, constant loving care, and masterful planning have made it so.

To select Beth El Memorial Park as the final resting place for your family will give you a deep sense of well-being in the knowledge that you have made the perfect choice. And to make your selection far prior to its need is to spare the living that ordeal in their hour of grief and utter distraction.

To act now would mean time . . . time to visit Beth El Memorial Park . . . time to make an unhurried, careful, thoughtful selection.

And finally, we remind you that there is a distinct advantage in the special price concession made to all members of Temple Emanu-El, Temple Israel, and Temple Beth El. Arrangements for payment over a period of years are easily made.

Your decision?

You may be sure that deciding to mail the card places you under no obligation.

Business Reply Card to Accompany Letter

BETH EL MEMORIAL PARK

Gentlemen:

I am interested in receiving further information and would like you to phone for an appointment

At my office ☐   Phone: _____

At my home ☐   Phone: _____

My Name _____

Address _____

I am a member of: Beth El ☐   Emanuel-El ☐
                                Israel ☐

Illustration B

I am writing to you as one who has recently become a member of Temple Beth El, on a subject of vital meaning and importance — Beth El Memorial Park, your synagogue's own cemetery.

Unfortunately, it is a fact that most people delay the purchase of proper burial grounds until the need for its use arises. This unwise delay invariably results in needless anguish at a time when one is emotionally upset.

I ask that you give immediate consideration to providing your family with suitable burial facilities, if you have not already done so. There is nothing morbid about the discussion of, or the decision to obtain, a permanent resting place for your loved ones. It is necessary, and if done long in advance of the need, much sorrow and strain can be avoided.

Please mail the enclosed card to Mr. Karl B. Segall, Managing Director of Beth El Memorial Park, who will be glad to give you complete details at your convenience.

Business Reply Card to Accompany Letter

BETH EL MEMORIAL PARK
Gentlemen:

I am interested in receiving further information and would like you to phone for an appointment

At my office ☐   Phone: _____

At my home ☐   Phone: _____

My Name_____

Address _____

I am a member of: Beth El ☐   Emanu-El ☐
                            Israel ☐

Each congregation should prepare an attractive brochure for its congregational cemetery and mail it once or twice a year to the membership. On the membership roster of most congregations there is one member who is in the advertising business. He is ready and willing to give you his professional guidance and advice as a service to his congregation, if you will call upon him. Use his expert knowledge and service and you will be the beneficiary of a professional job — a brochure you will be proud to distribute to your members and an assurance that it will receive attention. Samples of excellent cemetery brochures are available from the UAHC's Commission on Synagogue Administration.

Display Ads

The following are illustrations of display ads and notices in synagogue bulletins that have proven very effective:

TO IGNORE...

... the purchase of a family lot is to ignore the well-being and peace-of-mind of loved ones. For to delay such action is to impose upon yourself or a dear one a heart-breaking duty at a time when such matters should long since have been settled. Do not ignore this responsibility. Select a lot now in beautiful

BETH EL MEMORIAL PARK
For full details
phone TRinity 5-8530

NEGLECT...

...of so important a duty as the purchase of a family lot can cause untold hardship at a time when troubled minds cannot possibly do justice to so important a task. *Do it now.* Select a lot now in

BETH EL MEMORIAL PARK
For full details
phone TRinity 5-8530

TO EVADE...

... is not to perform. As head of your family, it is your duty to provide not only for today but for the future. The choice of a family plot is a task you should not delegate. It is one you cannot evade. The day of sorrow will have other claims upon your time. Visit beautiful *BETH EL MEMORIAL PARK* now and make your choice of a plot for your family.

Perpetual Care included in purchase price of every lot. Special discount to synagogue members. Term payments.

For full details
phone TRinity 5-8530

The following are examples of effective bulletin notices:

INSPECTION INVITED AT MEMORIAL PARK

The Anshe Emet Memorial Park Cemetery, located in Evanston, is a spot of verdant and enduring loveliness. Broad, tree-bordered driveways, winding roads, a natural lake, shrubbery and flowers in abundance form a picture of rare charm. A beautiful fountain, shaped in the form of a Mogen Dovid and exquisitely inscribed with fine Hebrew lettering, stands at the entrance to the cemetery.

Rare and good judgment was used in selecting the site for Memorial Park. Situated as it is on a ridge, high above the level of surrounding country, it enjoys the advantage of natural drainage. No effort or expense has been spared in creating a resting place of befitting quietude and beauty. Perpetual care is provided for in the sale of every burial space, with no additional charge to the owner.

Parking facilities at the older Jewish cemeteries at times are inadequate. In Memorial Park an owner may drive his car into the cemetery and park within a few feet of his space.

Lots can be purchased at the most reasonable prices, and on terms to suit the modest budget. A special insurance plan is offered, protecting the partial payment purchasers. There is no interest to pay, no taxes or special assessments, no handling charges of any kind.

Memorial Park is open for your inspection at all times. If you wish to have a representative of the congregation accompany you on an inspection tour, or if you desire further information, communicate with Mr. ———————————————, ——————————————— Street, STate 6740, or the synagogue office.

LIFE'S EVENTUALITIES

Our age is free of the hesitation and inhibitions of former days. We respectfully solicit your interest in the purchase of a plot in Union Field Cemetery. Our cemetery, with a tradition of almost eighty years of public service, is one of the finest and best managed burial organizations in the metropolitan area. All who have had occasion to visit its reverently-kept acres have gone away with the solacing assurance that here death is robbed of its sting.

We realize that it is wise and helpful to make preparations during the days of our life for the eventualities of our death and the passing of our loved ones. When the moment of emergency arrives, and it is an hour that each one of us has to face sooner or later, arrangements for interment may have to be made hurriedly. If you make plans beforehand, you are enabled to consider the whole question of "life in the house of peace" deliberately, intelligently, and with foresight. Rates are reasonable for four-, six-, eight-, and twelve-grave plots. For further information, call the synagogue office, ENdicott 2-0000, and ask for Mr. ——————————, our sexton.

LEO KEISER,
Cemetery Committee Chairman

While it is a source of much humor on occasion, the cemetery is an essential aspect of our religious life. It is, therefore, important that we be cognizant of our terminology in carrying out our responsibilities in promoting and administering the congregational cemetery. It would be wise to keep in mind the following public relations guide provided by the National Association of Cemeteries:

WATCH YOUR LANGUAGE

INURNMENT — This word should be used freely when discussing memorials. Rather than "putting them in a niche" or "Buying a niche" or "Getting an urn" or "Picking out a niche," say: "Selecting a memorial" or "Providing for the inurnment." *Don't say*: "We'll put the urn in the niche"; *say*: "We will *place* the memorial urn and the cremated remains in the niche" — *This is the Inurnment.*

INTERNMENT — is a word, but it does not apply to your business. It doesn't mean what you are trying to say. The word is *Interment.*

ENGRAVING — Refer to the name of the deceased as being "inscribed" on the memorial urn. This is the *inscription*. If you feel your families would better understand, say *lettering*.

DON'T SAY	SAY
Ashes	Cremated remains
Cheap	Economically or modestly priced, or inexpensive
Coffin	Casket
Corpse	Deceased or deceased person or your father, your husband, etc.
Engrave	Inscribe
Engraving	Inscription or lettering
Future use	Future need
Grave	Interment space or burial plot
Graveyard	Cemetery or memorial park
Headstone	Marker
Hearse	Funeral coach
Incinerate	Cremate
Incinerated remains	Cremated remains
Incineration	Cremation
Internment	Interment
Intombment	Entombment
Pallbearers	Casket bearers
Retort	Cremation chamber or cremation vault
Ship or mail	Send
Sold	Purchase
Storage	Care
Tombstone	Monument
Undertaker	Mortician or funeral director

REFERENCES

BRENNAN, R. L., *The Law Governing Cemetery Rules and Regulations,* Cemetery Legal Compass, Los Angeles.

FEDER, MAX, *Cemetery Operations and Procedures,* NATA-UAHC Synagogue Research Survey #5, UAHC, 1960.

FREEHOF, LOUIS J., *General Facts on the Community Mausoleum,* UAHC, 1958.

GORDON, J. J., *Cemetery Management,* Cemetery Beautiful Publishing Co., 1915.

JOHNSON, NOBLE, *Factors to Be Considered Before Starting a Mausoleum,* Proceedings, American Cemetery Association Convention, 1959.

MUCKLOW, WALTER, *Cemetery Accounts,* American Institute Publishing Co., 1935.

The Cemetery Handbook, Allied Arts Publishing Co., 1926.

WASSERMAN, DAVID, *The Jewish Cemetery in a Small Community,* UAHC's Synagogue Service, February, 1936.

WYRICK, RAY F., *Establishing a New Cemetery Involves Many Problems,* The American Cemetery, October, 1959.

CEMETERY ASSOCIATIONS

American Cemetery Association, Columbus, Ohio.

National Association of Cemeteries, Washington, D.C.

CEMETERY PUBLICATIONS

American Cemetery, New York, N.Y.

Cemetery Legal Compass, Los Angeles, Calif.

XIV The Synagogue
Staff

WE LIVE IN AN ERA OF SPECIALIZATION. OUR SOCIETY ACCEPTS THE
fact that in our personal lives, the business field, the professions,
or the area of religion, our world has become so complex that we
must call upon "experts" to assist us. This has become an accepted fact in the administration of our synagogues, as well. The synagogue has become all too encompassing to expect the rabbi to
serve as fiscal and administrative officer in addition to his religious, pastoral, and community functions. Even with a dedicated group of lay leaders, smaller congregations experience diffi-
culty and confusion when the synagogue does not have some professional and full-time paid assistance.

At the very least, a synagogue requires office personnel and
custodial help, creating a staff of two to four people in addition
to the rabbi. As a synagogue grows in membership and adds to
its physical facilities, the number of its clerical and maintenance
staff will increase proportionately. Generally there is a concomitant need for additional professional staff — teachers, religious
school principal, educator, choir, choirmaster, cantor, music director, youth and activities director, and a professional synagogue
administrator or, as he is frequently termed, an executive secretary or director.

The increase in synagogue staff members places a heavy responsibility upon the Board of Trustees of a religious institution.
In this day and age it is no longer possible to avoid the fact that
the synagogue now has an employer-employee relationship. It is
no longer accepted that the synagogue can utilize the fact that it
is a non-profit institution in this relationship. As a religious institution, it is charged with an overriding obligation to deal with
its employees in the context of the moral imperatives of the Jewish faith and to set an example for all to follow.

Since the stability and effectiveness of the synagogue and program will be related to the relative security and degree of con-
tentment of its staff, every congregation should have an estab-

lished personnel policy. To create, implement, and review this policy, the Board should establish a Personnel Committee. The members of this committee should consist of men and women who are knowledgeable in the area of personnel practices, familiar with the employment and working conditions prevalent in the community, and who are intimately involved with the administration and program of the congregation.

The major functions of the Personnel Committee are:

1. To establish and review at regular intervals the code of personnel practices and working conditions for the synagogue staff.

2. To review and make recommendations to the Board for the addition and elimination of staff.

3. To define the areas of responsibility for each staff position (Job Description and Analysis) and to set salary ranges and fringe benefits.

4. To recommend to the Board an adequate program of security against health and accident hazards and to provide retirement benefits for the staff.

5. To create a system for the handling of grievances and for their adjudication and resolution.

The importance of the work of the Personnel Committee in these five areas is highlighted by the fact that the synagogue has frequent changes in leadership, lay and rabbinic. Officers and Board members must change in the democratic nature of our society and its institutions, but the synagogue must and will continue to serve the needs of its membership. Its ability to continue to serve may well be measured by the stability of its staff and, therefore, it is essential that they have that sense of continuity and security which only a well conceived and fairly evaluated Code of Personnel Practices will provide.

The Role of the Rabbi

There are few better descriptions or definitions of the role of the rabbi in the contemporary synagogue than that postulated by Rabbi Jacob D. Schwarz. Although written many years ago, when

he was director of the UAHC-CCAR's Commission on Synagogue
Activities, it retains its relevancy:

> That the rabbi is not only the acknowledged, but confidential-
> ly expected to be, the leader in the synagogue may be taken
> for granted. His office is conceived in terms of such leader-
> ship and, however the definition of his qualification and
> function may differ, he is expressly chosen to be the embodi-
> ment and champion of the ideals and goals for which the
> synagogue stands. As such, he has certain definite responsi-
> bilities inherent in his task and, by the same token, the con-
> gregation which has so honored him, and its Board of Trus-
> tees, not to say every unit and agency within the synagogue,
> presumably working for the same ends, have equally definite
> obligations respecting him and his work.

It was discernible to Rabbi Schwarz that the rabbi's duties were
multiplying, that he was assuming more responsibilities never
before associated with the rabbinate, and that this presented
complex problems to the contemporary synagogue. It was not
only the question of a sufficient staff but, as he stated it, "What
are the essential labors which the rabbi must perform for the upbuilding of his congregation and what are his paramount duties
to his own people? . . . Can he surrender part of his leadership
without impairing the efficacy of his work as a whole?"

However, it is not our purpose to delve into this complicated,
evolving relationship but rather to establish some guidelines for
rabbi and lay leader alike in the area of administering the synagogue. The rabbi is titular leader of the synagogue by virtue of
his learning, his insight, and his example, and he has to earn his
high place in the estimation of the lay leaders, the staff, and the
membership.*

> In one respect our modern synagogues, with their elaborate
> physical plants, with many institutional features, with the
> multifarious organizations and groups which appear to be
> inseparable from our present-day life, and with the many

---

*The rabbi's role in the area of synagogue administration is well defined by Rabbi
Schwarz in his book, *Adventures in Synagogue Administration*.

problems of membership and finance which follow in their train, have added heavily to the rabbi's burden. In many congregations the administrative duties which fall to the lot of the rabbi because no other disposition has been made of them are entirely out of proportion to his constructive labors. To this administrative routine are frequently added, again by default of others by whom these duties should be properly assumed, the responsibility of increasing and maintaining membership, of conserving and supplementing income, and all the many burdensome duties of financial agent-in-chief.

It must be said that this situation has greatly improved in recent years. A growing number of congregations, especially the larger congregations, now have a paid executive secretary (synagogue administrator), an educational director, sometimes an activities director, and other executive and administrative personnel which relieve the rabbi of many routine duties. The more systematic handling of the membership and dues problem through the membership committee and through contact committees of the Board of Trustees has had a similar tendency. Since the qualifications for many of these tasks may be found in the Trustees and in other members of the congregation, it is the plain duty of the Board to organize these tasks accordingly.

While there may still be some argument about the role of the rabbi in the administrative aspects of the synagogue, statistics seem to indicate that a working partnership between rabbi, lay leaders, and professional administrator has evolved. In the vast majority of congregations the rabbi attends regularly meetings of the Board of Trustees. While no survey has been undertaken to determine the extent of the rabbi's participation in administration, Dr. Max Feder, past president of the National Association of Temple Administrators, points out that "it is now appreciated how important is the advice of the spiritual leader in the program and *administrative planning* of the synagogue."*

---

*UAHC-NATA Synagogue Research Survey #3 on *Temple Boards and Committees.*

The Professional Administrator

The professional, full-time synagogue administrator, known as *synagogue administrator, executive secretary, or executive director,* is a comparatively new functionary in the American synagogue. When the National Association of Temple Secretaries was founded in 1941, there were only a handful of these professionals. In 1962, the membership roster of the organization, now known as the National Association of Temple Administrators, an affiliate of the UAHC, numbered more than 150 men and women who are making a significant contribution to the growth and vitality of the Reform Jewish movement. There also exists a National Association of Synagogue Administrators (Conservative), organized in 1947, and now numbering close to 200 members.

It is recognized that large and even medium-sized congregations (500 or more members and/or an annual operating budget of $100,000 or more) can no longer be conducted on a purely voluntary basis. The time has also passed when the part-time, occasionally functioning secretary can do justice to the requirements of the contemporary synagogue. The conduct of the affairs of the modern synagogue requires the attention of a trained, full-time administrator, and a skill and technique all its own. Volunteer or part-time workers simply cannot give that alert, constructive service required to make the synagogue a compelling force, particularly in large communities. To bring the individual within the radius of synagogue influence, constructive planning is essential. Time, effort, and informed study of problems and situations are most necessary if the synagogue is to make its message and activities articulate and effective.

As the synagogue continues to expand its scope of activities and services to meet the needs of a more integrated and more mature Jewish community in America, as the functions of the synagogue multiply and take on new significance, the necessity for adequate organizational machinery, effectively conducted, becomes vital. By and large, our congregations have discarded the process of rule of thumb and the process of trial and error, and have introduced administrative knowledge and skills based upon research and tested experience.

Our lay leaders have come to realize that if the devotional and educational activities constitute the mind and soul of the synagogue, the administrative machinery represents its heart and circulatory system. Synagogue administration today has indeed become a science — a highly skilled process of informed and intelligent congregational management.

While the duties and responsibilities of the professional administrator will vary with each synagogue, the following are basic:

1. *Financial*
   a. Maintain and supervise the records according to established accounting and bookkeeping practice.
   b. Prepare and present periodic financial reports as required.
   c. Periodically review the expenses and income within the authorized budget.
   d. Render administrative direction and assistance in fundraising aspects as authorized by the Board of Trustees.

2. *Membership*
   a. Maintain accurate membership records which will reflect all pertinent data as to individuals and families.
   b. Assist in enrolling new members and the integration, orientation, and involvement of all members.

3. *Programming*
   a. Correlate and coordinate the efforts of all affiliate groups, as well as community organizations, as delineated by the Board and the rabbi.
   b. Schedule the use of facilities and maintain a calendar of events.

4. *Property and Equipment*
   a. Maintain the property of the synagogue in good condition.
   b. Make recommendations to the House Committee when extraordinary expenditures are required.
   c. Supervise the building custodian and maintenance staff to the end that the property and grounds are kept in such a state of cleanliness and appearance as befits a religious institution.
   d. Establish and maintain an accurate inventory of equipment and supplies and arrange for a schedule of replacement.

5. *Personnel*

   a. Establish personnel procedures and standards for all members of the staff, subject to Board approval. (This should cover vacations, hours of work, promotions, dismissals, leaves, etc.)

   b. Supervise the proper functioning of the staff in accordance with a table of organization.

   c. Provide for the social security coverage and other benefits as required by federal and state laws.

In order to fulfil creditably and effectively the challenges of his position, what should be the background of training and experience of the professional administrator?

1. He should possess a good Jewish education and background, including a reading knowledge of Hebrew, as well as an appreciation of the purposes and aims of the synagogue.

2. A knowledge of or experience in institutional finance and acquaintance with the sources of congregational income, tested fund-raising techniques, and the preparation and application of a planned budget are important.

3. A knowledge of office management and personnel practices and procedures.

4. Familiarity with the operation and maintenance of institutional buildings.

5. A background in institutional public relations and publicity.

6. He must be blessed with a gracious and personable disposition and the capacity to deal intelligently with individuals and groups. Studies in the fields of psychology and sociology will enable him to cope with the manifold problems of personal relationships in the congregation and the community at large.

7. A knowledge of group-work procedure and programming will enable him to assist in the many-faceted synagogue program.

A word about the relationship of the administrator to the rabbi. He must always bear in mind that the rabbi is the acknowledged head of the congregation and that nothing whatsoever in the life of the synagogue is outside the ken of the rabbi's knowledge and interest, though, in order to devote his time to the classic tasks of his calling, there are some departments of synagogue affairs to which he does not directly and specifically devote himself. On the other hand, the rabbi must recognize the broader function and key position which his administrator may occupy in the conduct of the affairs of the synagogue, and accord him the status of professional dignity commensurate with his calling.

Since the office of the synagogue administrator is the nerve center of all congregational activities, he must keep the rabbi fully posted on everything that transpires in his office, and there should be steady and regular contacts between them, a friendly interchange of ideas, and complete cooperation. Their relationship must be one of mutual understanding and confidence. There should be unanimity of purpose and aim.

The Administrator and the Board

The synagogue may be compared to a watch, with the Board of Trustees as the stem, the rabbi and administrator as the two main wheels or gears, and the hands representing activity and results. The stem in winding the spring is the motivating force. The action of the gears is dependent upon the spring. In turn the motion of the hands is continued or arrested by the movement of the gears. We see here a mutual interdependence — a complete harmony. The Board must be the activating and guiding force. The primary province of the rabbi is the religious and educational welfare of his congregants. The administrator is the specialist in synagogue management. His function is not only to deal with the practical aspects of the synagogue, but to integrate more effectively the working mechanism of the entire synagogue structure and to lend constructive aid to each component part of the synagogue program.

The relationship of the administrator to the Board of Trustees must, of course, be one of mutual understanding and confidence. He must not be regarded as a glorified secretary or bookkeeper or even an executive sexton, but must be accorded a status of professional dignity commensurate with his important function in the synagogue. He must not be regarded as a financial wizard who makes deficits disappear by a mere wave of his wand and pulls memberships out of a hat. The administrator is entitled to certain elementary privileges. Paramount, of course, is a living wage which will insure physical and mental comfort and at the same time be productive of the best in the man. He needs rest and relaxation each week, a reasonable vacation period, time to spend on a hobby or two, read a newspaper and book, participate in civic affairs if he chooses to do so, take a course at the university to broaden himself, and attend meetings of professional workers in his field. By virtue of his position, the administrator must be vested by the Board with authority equal to his responsibilities. If tasks are set forth, the wherewithal for their accomplishment must also be supplied. As one cannot expect a woodsman to be efficient with a dull ax so one cannot expect action on the part of the administrator who, among other things, is hampered by a lack of funds or adequate clerical help. Tenure, or security of position, is another major factor. Tenure, however, is more than a signed contract. It envisions an enlightened Board, alive to its duties and responsibilities.

To do a proper job, the administrator must absorb and be in complete sympathy with the ideology of his congregation. Once policies are established by the Board, it is his responsibility to see that they are carried out. He must even be willing to submerge his personality in its interests. Among other things he must be a judge of human nature, a man of humor, patience, and optimism. He must command respect by confidence in his own ability to do the job that confronts him. He must be able to accept inevitable rebukes for mistakes of omission or commission; place the synagogue and its principles above personal and partisan pressure. He must, within the powers and duties outlined for him by the Board, so apply skill, resourcefulness, ingenuity, and intelligence as to insure the fullest utility of the physical resources of the synagogue and the greatest cooperation of the human element.

There must be a human relationship between the administrator and the Board. They ought to respect each other and approve each other's motives, methods, and purposes. The administrator must keep his Board closely informed on all aspects of every problem confronting the synagogue. On the other hand, no Board which makes a pretense at good relationships with the administrator will withhold information it is his business to have.

Conclusion

The synagogue administrator, to truly serve his calling, must be constantly alert to the creative endeavors of other congregations, must participate in the work of his professional organization, and be cognizant of the aids available from the national institutions with which his congregation is affiliated. He must be familiar with other national and international Jewish organizations so that he can judge their effects upon the program of his own congregation. A qualified, religiously-oriented, and culturally enthusiastic synagogue administrator can be a vital asset to the lay and rabbinic leadership of the congregation and can enrich the life of the entire synagogue membership.

REFERENCES

Careers in Synagogue and Temple Administration, B'nai B'rith Vocational Service, 1959.

Conducting Workshops and Institutes, Adult Education Association of the U.S.A.

Howse, W. L., *The Church Staff and Its Work,* Broadman Press, 1959.

The Temple Administrator, NATA, 1959.

Index

A

ABC of Synagogue Administration, The, 23-24

Academy of Pumbedita, 6

Academy of Sura, 6

Accident and Health Insurance, 120

Actors' Synagogue, 3

Address, change of (keeping records up to date), 112

ADLER, ROBERT S., 88, 89

Administration of synagogue, by Board of Trustees, 9-10, 11, 12-15, 17-19 (*charts*), 22-55; organizational structure, 17-19 (*charts*); basic principles, 20-21; committee system, 37-51; building program committees, 97-98, 100-101; office management, 104-114; building construction and maintenance, 116-138 (*charts*); membership factor, 139-156 (*charts*); public relations and publicity, 157-163; congregational cemetery, 165-180; synagogue staff, 181-188

Administrator, professional, 185-188; duties and responsibilities, 186-187; relationship to rabbi, 187-188, relationship to Board of Trustees, 188

Adult Education Committee, 45

Adventures in Synagogue Administration, 183

Affiliate Organizations Committee, 49

Aliyo, 56

ALTMAN, JOSEPH, 88

Amendments, as provided for by synagogue's constitution, 17

American Jewish Archives, 8

American Jewish Historical Society, 8

American Protestantism, influence on functions of the rabbi, 9

American Synagogue, 8-11

American Synagogue for Today and Tomorrow, An, 117

American Synagogue, The — A Progress Report, 118

Ancient administration of synagogues, 4

Anniversaries, significant, recording of, 113

Annual reports, 110

Anshe Emet Synagogue, Chicago, 90, 177

Architects' Advisory Panel, UAHC, 97, 117

Archives Committee, 51

Ashkenazic synagogues in America, 8, 9

Attendance at Worship Committe, 47

Audit, of congregation's books, 109

Automobile Liability Insurance, 120

Auxiliary Affiliate Groups, as provided for by synagogue's constitution, 17

Auxiliary Organizations and Departments, related to committee structure and function, 49-50

B

Babylonian exile, synagogues during, 3

BALLENGER, A. G., 89

Bar Mitzvah, recording of, 113

BARON, MURRAY, 84

Beneficiary of insurance policies, synagogue named as, 80

"Bequeaths $9,000,000," 94-95

Bequest and Capital Gifts Committee, 41-42

Bequests to synagogue, 80

BERGMAN, RABBI LEO, 91

BERLINER, SAMEL, 10

Bes Chayim (House of Life), 164

Bes din (court), 5, 7

Bes ha-k'neses (House of Assembly), 13

Commission on

SYNAGOGUE
ADMINISTRATION

**of the Union of American Hebrew Congregations
and Central Conference of American Rabbis**

AS OF 1963

Dr. Harold M. Faigenbaum, Chairman

Myron E. Schoen, Director

Rabbi Stanley R. Brav
Dr. Max Feder
Mr. Julian Feldman
Dr. Samuel Fox
Dr. Henry J. Gewirtzman
Dr. Milton Gipstein
Rabbi Theodore H. Gordon
Mr. Irving I. Katz
Rabbi Jacob Polish
Mr. Emanuel M. Rosenthal
Mr. Victor Ross
Mr. Edward Starin

Rabbi Maurice N. Eisendrath, UAHC, Ex-Officio

Rabbi Albert G. Minda, CCAR, Ex-Officio

Rabbi Sidney L. Regner, CCAR, Ex-Officio

About
the Authors

For more than 35 years, IRVING I. KATZ has served as administrator of Congregation Beth El in Detroit. A pioneer in his profession and a recognized authority in all facets of synagogue work, he was organizer and first president of the National Association of Temple Administrators, an affiliate of the Union of American Hebrew Congregations. As honorary president of the NATA, he lectures frequently at seminaries and conventions of Jewish organizations. In addition to his many published works on synagogue administration, he is the author of several historical monographs, including *The Jewish Soldier from Michigan in the Civil War*, published by Wayne University Press.

MYRON E. SCHOEN is director of the Commission on Synagogue Administration of the Union of American Hebrew Congregations and the Central Conference of American Rabbis. Prior to coming to the UAHC he served as administrator of the Stephen Wise Free Synagogue in New York and as assistant to the National Director of the B'nai B'rith Hillel Foundations. With a background in economics, business administration, and personnel management, he serves the NATA as a member of its Executive Board and director of the Placement Service. Since 1960, Mr. Schoen has been editor of the Synagogue and School Management section of the *National Jewish Post and Opinion*, and contributes a weekly column on synagogue problems. He is secretary of the UAHC's Architects Advisory Panel and the Board of Certification for Temple Administrators of the UAHC, CCAR, and NATA.